DELIVER US FROM EVIL

The Remarkable True Story of a Child's Abuse, Spiritual Deception, Deliverance and Ultimate Redemption

By Ron Corcoran

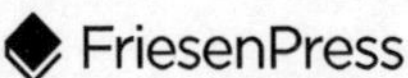

Suite 300 - 990 Fort St
Victoria, BC, V8V 3K2
Canada

www.friesenpress.com

First Edition — 2016

ISBN
978-1-4602-8990-7 (Hardcover)
978-1-4602-8991-4 (Paperback)
978-1-4602-8992-1 (eBook)

1. BIOGRAPHY & AUTOBIOGRAPHY

Distributed to the trade by The Ingram Book Company

If you have read Scott Peck's *People of the Lie*, as I have, and have been shocked by the depth of human evil, you have seen nothing yet. Ron's childhood was unremitting evil. It is compelling reading, knowing how healthy, warm and kind Ron is. It is miraculous that someone could come through so much adversity and yet be able to have had a successful ministry for over thirty years. I could not put the book down. This is epic and needs to be read by everyone; it is shocking and remarkable. God has redeemed his life. I am so grateful to call this man my very good friend.

Rt. Rev. Dr. Trevor H. Walters
Suffragan Bishop for Western Canada
Author of EAS Syndrome

From despair and depression to freedom and forgiveness—what a faith-inspiring, hope-giving story! Ron takes the reader on his painful journey of horrendous, multiple abuse, but does not leave us there. He shows us his path to faith and invites us to join him on this life-changing experience. Ron models the necessity and power of forgiveness in the healing process and provides Biblical scholarship and insight. We are encouraged to share in his triumph over trials and tragedy, to pursue help and healing for our own hurts and to join in the celebration of God's love and life for everyone. It was a privilege to walk alongside Ron for part of his healing journey.

Becca C. Johnson, Ph.D., Licensed Psychologist
Dr. Johnson works with the abused and exploited, and provides trauma care training worldwide. She is the author of Good Guilt, Bad Guilt *(1996) and co-authored* Overcoming Emotions that Destroy *(2009) with Pastor Chip Ingram. Dr. Johnson currently serves as the Clinical Director of Engedi Refuge, a residential program for sexually exploited women, and also as Consulting Psychologist for AIM (Agape International Mission).*

This is a forthright book written by a courageous man. Ron lived through horrific abuse and dared revisit it and write about it. In this book, Ron shares with us what he most desperately needed—the healing, restoration and transformation of his body, soul and spirit—and how he received it. Ron has been a friend and brother in Christ for almost thirty years and I have been privileged to see God working this miracle in him. God continues to repay Ron the years the locusts have eaten. This book is an inspiring description of God's healing grace, and an encouragement for anyone struggling with forgiveness.

Jean Hamilton
Senior Counsellor, New Brunswick Branch Office
The Isaiah 40 Foundation
www.isaiah40foundation.org

Battered, bruised, broken, abused and shattered—this is one man's story of how he overcame by God's saving Grace and how he made Jesus the Lord of this life, even through all the pain and suffering he endured.

Alison Chambers
Friend for over forty years

Having known Ron for almost thirty years, and having been appalled and aghast at the circumstances of his life story, I am both amazed and pleased to read this book and see how he has turned a grievous situation into such a story of redemption and hope. Rather than living under a cloud of justified un-forgiveness and resentment, Ron is living in total freedom—truly a miracle of God's grace.

Rev. Don Hamilton
Rector, Christ the Redeemer Anglican Church

Ron's book, *Deliver Us From Evil*, is truly a gem. For those who have endured childhood abuse and neglect, Ron's personal story will provide hope not only for this life, but for eternity. Ron is a gifted teacher/preacher whom I've known close to thirty years. He is a man of his word—one whom I trust implicitly. I love the overall theme that God is faithful and uses tough times to shape and mould us. I am inspired by this story that teaches us to seek and keep our heart right before the Lord, and the power of Christ to transform our lives.

Chris Hornibrook
Leadership Mentor
President, The Master's Program in Canada
http://canada.mastersprogram.org

Ron Corcoran is a man of Heroic faith. His fruitful life of ministry and his Christ like spirit provide clear evidence of a life deeply rooted in the heart of Jesus. I know this about Ron. What I didn't know before reading this book was the extent of evil unleashed upon Ron throughout the formative years of his life. I found the accounts of the depth and breadth of abuse to be astounding. But what I found even more astounding was the super-abundant grace of God that so gloriously redeemed Ron. Ron's life is an open book journey to wholeness. His story will bring inspiration and hope to all who read it.

Rev. Dr. Gary Bennett, Pastor
Victoria First Church of the Nazarene

There is a transparency and honesty in these pages that I have rarely found in any book I have read. This is a book that likely has affected every emotion in my being. It is an extraordinary testimony of the grace and tenderness of the Lord, amidst the trauma and pain often inflicted by a world ignorant of God's saving grace. Ron Corcoran has described his early years with a candour that could only be adequately addressed through the power of the Cross of Christ. In these pages, Ron has identified with the plight of humanity in terms of identity and purpose and has suffered the consequences of the worst the world can throw at us—even from birth. Ron Corcoran is living proof that God is able to do far more than we could ever possibly ask or think. He is the God of Transformation—and this book is living proof that nothing is impossible with Him (c.f. Luke 1:37).

Ron has experienced the unfairness of a fallen world and has learned how to address the "silence of God." In so doing, he has lived out the reality and promise of Scripture, and his testimony is proof that there is hope and purpose for every human being, no matter how distant and improbable that may feel at times. The pages of this book are both transparent and dramatic, and through them those with many unanswered questions will find a refuge of hope.

Rev. Dr. Alistair P. Petrie
Executive Director, Partnership Ministries
partnershipministries.org

Be warned. You will need to pray your way through the first chapters of this book. Ron Corcoran takes us on his horrific journey from infancy through adulthood—a journey that causes one to scream "enough!" as the saga of relentless abuse constantly confronts the reader. It is also a journey from abuse and doubt to love and redemption—a modern Damascus Road encounter. This most godly man has transcended his traumatic history—a history that shaped and miraculously enriched Ron's spiritual life and inspired urgency in sharing his faith.

Wendy and Craig Davis
Retired Social Worker and Educator

The cruel and devastating effects of childhood abuse are graphically described in this highly personal account of Ron Corcoran's informative years. In the wake of anger, mistrust, poor judgment and ultimately despair, Ron discovers God's deep love, grace and the road to redemption. His personal growth in thirty-five years of lay and ordained ministry has been a remarkable journey, but true freedom has been found in knowing God's forgiveness—and the joy of forgiving those who so nearly destroyed him.

Dr. Chris Muller
MB ChB

This book is dedicated to my beloved wife
Deirdre Corcoran

You have indeed shown me a place where dreams come true!

CONTENTS

DELIVER US FROM EVIL

Deliver — to set free, to be liberated or to be rescued

Evil — something that brings sorrow, distress or calamity, the fact of suffering...wrongdoing, morally reprehensible, sinful, wicked

Redeem — to buy back, to free from what distresses or harms, to free from captivity by payment of ransom, to change for the better, to restore, to free from the consequences of sin.[1]

1 Merriam — Webster, *Webster's Ninth New Collegiate Dictionary,* 1984, pp, 336, 430, 986

ACKNOWLEDGEMENTS

This, my third book, has been the most challenging to write, but I have had much support. I would like to thank Don and Jean Hamilton who gave me the use of their apartment on the Northumberland Strait in New Brunswick in the fall of 2014. It was a perfectly peaceful setting in which to begin this difficult work.

My very patient editors, Lynne and Mike Damant, have reviewed, prayed through and encouraged me through all eleven drafts of this book. I pray that God will reward them for their outstanding work. Thank you for your constant prayer support, patience, love and fellowship as we laboured together. Bless you both!

A huge thank-you to my friend Bill Cozens who worked with me for weeks trying to find the *right* cover; Bill, you are a saint of the highest order. Keith and Kayh, N and C and my little friend Joshua, came to my rescue. The cover speaks volumes. Bless all of you for your help in this endeavour.

To my friends at FriesenPress, especially Genevieve, Colin and Oriana, who helped get this book into print. A special thank you to Renée Layberry from FriesenPress, for her editing and sensitivity in handling such a difficult topic; I will not forget your grace and encouragement.

When I began writing this book, I intended dedicating it to the men and women who over the years have been 'father' and 'mother' figures to me. The list is far too long, but you and God know who you are. Some have gone into glory, but I have not forgotten them and I look for a great and glorious reunion one day. So many others continue to walk with me day by day and moment by moment – thank you!

I sent the initial draft of the book to ten people seeking their endorsement. Their positive responses gave me the grace and courage to carry on. I give very special thanks to Dr. Becca Johnson and Kandy Stephenson as they were instruments of God's grace as I moved from depression and despair to deliverance and redemption. It would not have happened without their expertise, professional skills, wisdom and love. Words are inadequate to describe my appreciation.

Gradwell, you and I know that this book would not have been printed without your gracious gift. May what you have done in secret be rewarded in ways that you cannot imagine.

Grateful thanks to my darling and noble wife Deirdre. Deirdre, you make me a better person in so many ways. Your prayers, support and encouragement light up my life and sixteen years later, you are still the apple of my eye and my strong tower in times of difficulty and challenge. Bless you for saying 'Yes' to me all those years ago. My only wish is that we had met decades earlier! Thank you for loving me!

Last, but very first in my heart my Lord and Saviour Jesus Christ. Thank you for delivering me from evil and filling me with your abundant Grace. You paid my ransom and I have been redeemed. St. Paul was right when he described you as the indescribable gift.[1] There are not enough words in any language that could ever express my gratitude.

---

1 2 Corinthians 9:15

Soli Deo Gloria:

To God alone be the glory

FOREWORD

This book discloses a tragedy of abuse—but more importantly it is a journey of overcoming.

I first met Ron Corcoran in June of 1995, in my professional capacity as a clinical counsellor. He presented with issues relating to guilt, abandonment, failure and a need to forgive. As we worked together, the heartbreaking years of abuse by family members, from the time he was a little boy into adulthood, were revealed. As a therapist I had heard many clients recount their own sad and devastating stories of abuse. But with Ron, I was aghast and horrified by the relentless years of abuse he endured at the hands of some family members who should have cherished, loved and encouraged this little boy into manhood. As Ron was finally getting on his feet, he was once again betrayed by an elaborate spiritual deception from those who claimed to love him. How did he survived to become a productive member of society?

Over the course of many months, Ron and I worked to help him begin to live more freely from his past. We examined his role in his family of origin and it became clear he carried a sense of responsibility for everything that had gone wrong. In his mind, the abuse by family must have been because he was not good enough. He then carried this sense of responsibility into his adulthood, career, and personal relationships. He carried an inordinate burden of guilt over any failure.

Most profound, however, was the freedom Ron began to experience as he accepted that his Heavenly Father forgave him. As a priest, Ron readily accepted that others were forgiven for any and all of their wrongdoing, but he struggled to accept the same forgiveness. He eventually did, but it was an agonizing, soul-searching process. When he accepted the forgiveness of God, he was then able to move toward forgiving his family members for all the years of pain and grief. Ron had worked extremely hard, dealing with very difficult issues, and our sessions came to a close.

Many years later, Ron met and married Deirdre. Our relationship shifted from one of therapist and client to friends. I am now privileged to call both Ron and Deirdre friends. A few months ago, as his friend, Ron asked me to read his book and perhaps make some comments. As I began to read, I was filled with sorrow to again be privy to the pain, injustice, shame and constant abuse to which he had been subjected. When I first heard his story, as his therapist, his recounting of events were often separated by a week or more until we met for our next counselling session. However, this time, as I tried to read his story all in one sitting, I was overwhelmed with grief at what my friend had had to endure. I started to question whether he should publish this very vulnerable account of his life. I was concerned he was exposing himself to more hurt and pain as readers, some of them friends and family, saw his vulnerability.

As I continued reading, the words of the Apostle Paul, as found in Romans 8:35–37, came to me: "Who shall separate us from the love of Christ? Shall trouble or hardship or persecution or famine or nakedness or danger or sword? No, in all these things we are more than conquerors through Him who loved us." In my understanding, being more than a conqueror means to overcome the challenges that face us in this world through the love of Christ. In my counselling career I have seen many people who, through no fault of their own, have not been able to overcome the impact of guilt and abuse. One of the many privileges Ron and Deirdre have afforded me is a greater wisdom and experience to help those individuals to become "conquerors" too. I am a better counsellor, Christian, and friend for knowing Ron.

I realized that while Ron is a survivor of abuse, he is predominantly, through Christ, more than a conqueror! Through his abusive past and history of abandonment and betrayal, Ron was never separated from the love of Christ. Christ's love may, at times, have been buried under his pain. However, this trouble and hardship have led Ron to this place of writing a book, and sharing his journey. His story of survival and transformation is an inspiration to others who have suffered and a prescription for healing and renewal. I invite you to read and discover how one man, with the love and encouragement of his Saviour, was able to overcome his abusive past and truly forgive.

May Our Lord say: "Well done, good and faithful servant."

Kandy Stephenson
M.T.S.C.
Registered Clinical Counsellor

INTRODUCTION

Victor Frankl, in his great work, '*Man's Search for Meaning*'[2] wrote, "Forces beyond your control can take away everything you possess except one thing, your freedom to choose how you will respond to the situation. You cannot control what happens to you in life, but you can always control what you will *feel* and *do* about what happens to you."

I want you to know from the beginning of this book that I messed up my life. As you read, you will discover that there were many factors — childhood abuse and adult spiritual deception, which significantly contributed to that mess. When things happened to me I often did not or could not control my feelings and took actions that had long lasting and life changing consequences. The book is about my struggles and my recovery. At times, it will be hard to read.

Words were not sufficient to describe the extreme agony and soul searching I went through when I decided it was time to write this book. Some of the narrative is about tremendous suffering, but it is also a chronicle of incredible deliverance and redemption. Before you start, I want you to know that the first part of the book is rooted in pain, fear, cruelty, torment, betrayal, despair, hopelessness and even hatred. The story then changes to

2 Victor E. Frankl, *Man's Search For Meaning, pp. x*

one of deliverance and redemption, deliverance and redemption that came through the mercy, love and healing grace of God.

The story then again changes from one of redemption to one of tremendous betrayal and spiritual manipulation of the worst kind. I fell into an abyss and it took me almost fourteen years to finally be set free. Then my chronicle of deliverance and redemption is revived once more. Again, God manifested life to me in the overwhelming love shown to me by those considered by many to be very ordinary people. But, for me, they remain my mentors and my heroes.

Although the events I relate in this book may at times seem unbelievable, they are true and accurate. They have not been embellished or exaggerated in any way. To protect the dignity and privacy of others, I have taken the liberty of changing their names.

When I was a child, I thought I was all alone in a world filled with fear, sorrow, and endless remorse. When I became an adult, I discovered I was not alone. There are thousands of abused children—and yes, there are also thousands of abused adults who have never been able to deal or at times cope with the trauma that happened to them as children. Many abuse victims believe they can hide their past deep inside themselves, but they do not realize that the previous abuse will manifest itself in their day-to-day living. Some believe that, if they ignore the demons and darkness within, it will all go away. Therefore, they do everything in their power to keep the Pandora's Box closed. But the lid strains to push its way open.

I offer this book with the prayer and hope that those with whom it resonates may find within these pages their own hope, deliverance and redemption. I am writing for those who have been severely wounded and have wondered if anyone could ever love them. I write for those who have been abused physically, mentally, sexually, verbally and spiritually. I write so that others may realize that they are not alone in their suffering; there are many who do understand. Others have walked through similar valleys of suffering in order to find and then climb to the mountaintop of wholeness.

You may find the first steps may be frightening, but I invite you to take my hand in yours and let me walk with you, until you are ready to travel alone. I know that if you decide to climb to the top of the mountain, you will discover within yourself a heart that is unconquerable, a heart that refuses to submit any longer to a life of darkness and despair. Instead, your heart will reach up to find the light of life. Then you will know that it is safe to place your hand permanently in the hand of the One who loved you long before you knew He even existed.

Part I

GATES OF HELL

February 7, 1953 – May 29, 1979

“May the day of my birth perish,
And the night that said, ‘A boy is conceived!’
That day — may it turn to darkness;
May God above not care about it
May no light shine on it.
May gloom and utter darkness
Claim it once more;
May a cloud settle over it;
May blackness overwhelm it.
That night — may thick darkness seize it;
May it not be included among the days of the year
Nor be entered in any of the months.
Why did I not perish at birth,
And die as I came from the womb?”
(Job 3:3–6 & 11)

PROLOGUE
In The Beginning

I heard the footsteps as she rapidly moved down the hall, and I did everything I could to shake myself awake. I'd trained myself to listen for her footsteps, but on this morning, I just couldn't wake up. I'd been up again in the middle of the night to rock the baby to sleep, and so I was totally exhausted. I knew what would happen if I was not up at the side of the bed by the time she arrived. But I was too late, and the kicking with her hard shoes began, with one blow after another.

"Get out of bed, you useless thing!" she shouted. "You will *never* amount to anything! Get out of bed and clean up this house before you go to school—and if you don't have it done, you are *not* going to school. You will spend the day with me, and I will teach you not to be lazy!"

The kicks continued to assault me as I lay on the lower bunk bed, which had been mine for almost nineteen years. I tried to protect my kidneys and my private parts, and I cried out as kick after kick landed on my chest and legs. Perhaps if I cried loudly enough, someone would hear and come to my rescue, but my siblings who slept in the same room carried on pretending to be asleep. How did I know they were pretending? Her yelling and my crying made enough noise to wake the dead. Not that it would have made any difference; it seemed that nothing could stop her. The monster was loose, and another day dawned in my world of hell.

I call her "the monster" even though she was my biological mother; after all, she gave me birth. I am one of thirteen children; I was the eighth in a family of ten boys and three girls. I was the fifth boy, and five more boys were born after me. The average gap between most of us was seventeen months, except for two sisters who were born eleven months apart.

I was the last child born in Summerside, Prince Edward Island. Shortly after my birth, we moved to Greenwood, Nova Scotia, and then to Sydney, Nova Scotia. Those who are familiar with Canada's armed forces will recognize that all these places were Air Force stations. My father had served in the Second World War, and after the war he returned to Prince Edward Island to farm. Family members say my father hated farming, and so decided to rejoin the military and carry on with the work he had done during the war as a military policeman. At the end of my father's military career we moved to Ottawa, Ontario, where my three oldest siblings had settled.

My mother, who was a member of a large family, was carrying my father's child when they married just before the start of the Second World War. My oldest brother was born in 1939, and the next boy was born in 1941 after my father had left for overseas. The remaining eleven children came after the war and the youngest when my mother was forty-eight years old. There is a five-year gap between my two youngest brothers.

Before I go into the details of my upbringing, I need to share with you that I am very aware of how difficult it must have been to raise thirteen children. At times it must have stretched my parents to the outer limits to provide food, clothing and shelter for all of us. But that burden could never justify the excessive punishment and the absolute cruelty that took place in our home.

How would I describe my parents and my relationship with them? When I think of them as individuals whom I would describe, I would initially say that my father was six feet tall and a very handsome man, and my mother was about five foot seven and a very attractive woman. When they were all dressed up to go out for an evening, they made a striking couple. But when it comes to describing my relationship with my parents, I would have to admit that I didn't have a relationship with either of them, as I truly did not know them. Yes, I lived with my parents for the first nineteen years of my life, and they did indeed raise me, but I can honestly say I did not know them—and they certainly did not know me. I cannot tell you about their personal relationship, and I cannot tell you why one parent did the things she did or why the other seemingly turned a blind eye to the awful things that took place in our home.

When I was born, my father was thirty-six years old, and the image of him that remains in my mind is that he always seemed old. He did not talk about his war service, but my older siblings said that he had broken his back in a motorcycle accident while serving overseas. He recovered in a London hospital and then rejoined the war effort. I remember hearing through the family grapevine that when he returned from the war, my father said to my mother, "You will have to discipline the children as I don't want to do anything that would injure them."

When I say that I thought he was old, I could not help but notice that he carried himself as if he had a huge weight on his shoulders. When I was a child, I thought the weight of that burden was the responsibility of caring for thirteen children, but as an adult, I believe it was not only that, but also the toll the war years had taken on him—emotionally, physically, and mentally. Some of my siblings describe my father as a kind man, and some would also say that he sincerely loved them. Many of them would say that they had a good relationship with him. As I observed his interactions with my older and younger siblings, the relationship with them seemed to be loving and warm.

On the other hand, my memory of him is the exact opposite. I found my father very cold and shallow towards me. My father died in the fall of 1987. After his funeral my family sat around in my brother's living room talking about how kind, loving, gentle and fun my father was. I wanted to scream, "Who are you talking about?" I honestly do not remember any particular kindnesses or affection either from my father to me or from me to my father. I remember only one meaningful conversation I had with him in thirty-five years, which I will share with you in chapter nine of this book.

As a child I was so afraid of him that I avoided him as much as possible. He seemed to have nothing to say to me and, quite frankly, I lived in terror of him. Every time my mother beat me, my father would blame me for upsetting her. Then he would spend time chastising me and, when he was done, would banish me from his presence with his familiar refrain of "Get out of my sight." I don't recall him asking me to share my side of the story. Even if he'd asked (which he didn't), I already knew I couldn't speak the truth, because if I dared to defend myself I would get another beating as soon as he left for work the next morning. In this family of thirteen children, I felt like I was the lost one. I truly believed that in this family, I had no place. I didn't belong.

To save money, every month we would take turns in the bathroom and my father would shave our heads, so we didn't look like hippies. But that is the only time I ever remember my father putting his hands on me—except periodically when he was dishing out corporal punishment. While he was cutting my hair, I kept praying that he would hurry up so I could flee from his presence. In addition, even though it was my mother who carried out ninety percent of the corporal punishment, we always lived with the threat of "Just wait until your father gets home." It seemed as if I was beaten every day, and so there was a complete lack of joy in waiting for my father to come home. He wouldn't protect me from the monster. Whenever my father interacted with me, he always referred to me as "the runt," and although he may have from time to time been teasing, I despised that nickname. Consequently, I didn't have a parent I could go to for counsel or understanding. I had no place of safety and no reason to trust either of them.

The basic truth was that my father was a stranger to me, as I was to him. We would pass each other in the hallway of our home, but it was like strangers passing each other on a dark night. We had nothing to say to each other, and consequently I would say we had no real relationship. Our connection for the most part was non-existent, and I have no meaningful recollections to use as a baseline to describe a genuine relationship with him. I fearfully respected him, because he was my father, but I don't ever remember warm feelings of love to him from me or from him to me. When I think about feelings toward each other,

I would have to say that for the most part we were indifferent to each other.

Over the years I have read a number of books and articles on unjust suffering. Auschwitz survivor and Nobel Prize winner Elie Wiesel wrote, "The opposite of love is not hate. It's indifference."[3] I think my father was indifferent to me and I could never get close to him. In the clothes that I was forced to wear around the house for years, I felt nothing but shame when I came into his presence, and I think it embarrassed him that the monster was forcing me to wear such clothes. I firmly believe that my presence could not help but remind him that things were not well on the home front. Yes, there is no doubt that the word *non-existen*t is absolutely accurate to describe my relationship with my father, and indifferent is how we felt toward each other.

On the other hand, my mother was not a stranger, and from age four to nineteen I viewed her as a monster. It took many, many years and hundreds of hours of counselling for the monster to finally lose her grip on my soul. With thirteen children to raise and one pregnancy after another, my mother, for the most part, was a homemaker. As an adult, I have concluded that my mother suffered from postpartum depression that at times sent her completely off the deep end. From 1946 to 1958, my mother was either pregnant (11 times) or recovering from a pregnancy. Her body had no chance to recover completely between births. In 1963, when she was forty-eight, and five years after her last pregnancy, she gave birth to her thirteenth child.

For a time, when we lived in Sydney, my mother was also a substitute schoolteacher and she ran the snack bar at the local recreation centre. I don't remember ever having her as a substitute teacher in one of my classes, and I wasn't permitted to go to the snack bar at the recreation centre. I was happy when my

3 *U.S. News and World Report*, 27 October 1986

mother was substituting or working at the snack bar, because I didn't fear coming home for lunch since she was not there. Furthermore, those were the days that my brother Joseph and I removed ourselves from the steps and ran and played freely. (I will tell you more about the steps in chapter three.)

Today I remain convinced that if my mother had been born in a later generation, she would have been a career woman, as she had been trained to be a teacher. Sadly, I don't think my mother realized the opportunities she dreamed of when she started out in life. Instead she was burdened with caring for thirteen children, and I think she went through life overwhelmed with that responsibility. Most of the encounters I had with my mother were violent and loveless. When I was younger she used shoes, belts, hands and fists as her weapons of punishment. However, when I got older, the weapons changed. Seeing the fire in her eyes when she meted out punishment, I had no doubt she hated me. Consequently, I feared her, and over time I also grew to hate her. I have never understood why my mother hated me, but she also displayed the same violence and loveless attitude towards two of her other children: my older sister Cynthia and my older brother Joseph. All three of us received the brunt of her anger and cruelty. Hatred repeatedly appeared to motivate her vicious attacks against us on an almost daily basis. I believe that this is an unacknowledged truth in our family, although to this day it remains unspoken and very rarely, if ever, alluded to. Once in a while the lid lifts off Pandora's Box, and truths from the past spill out. However, my siblings immediately close the box before too much is revealed to brothers-in-law, sisters-in-law or nephews and nieces who may be present. No, what went on in our house is a filthy family secret that to this day still holds many of my family members in bondage.

Mother did not tolerate the three of us and for the most part acted as if she loathed us. We were the recipients of the awful abuse she doled out, it seemed, every day of our lives. I choose the word *loathe* specifically as her violent outbursts cannot be described any other way. I do not understand why she hated us so much and probably never will. It is awful to realize that the person who gave you birth actually hates you. In fact, I would have to say that there was no indication that she ever loved me. However, many years ago, I came to accept this fact as part of my history. If I had to testify before a court of law about my upbringing, I could easily say that my mother hated me, my sister, and my brother. They would have to give their own testimony, but I would base my testimony on my mother's daily behaviour towards me from age four to nineteen.

Even in her latter years, she lived in total denial that she hated or did any lasting harm to any one of us. Her relationship with my two siblings and me was one of discord, fits of uncontrolled rage and, at times, her behaviour would easily be described by outsiders as absolutely evil. One of the things that my mother was extremely careful about was not letting others see this dark side of her personality. Her face, her manner and her voice could change in an instant. It was amazing to observe. It was not only the awful beatings or evil actions I remember so vividly, but also the degrading, vicious, malicious words she constantly hurled at me, such as, *"Runt," "Good for nothing," "You will never amount to anything," "Can't you do anything right?" "You are failure and you will always be a failure!"* Those words reverberated in my heart and mind for years and years. The children's nursery rhyme that says: "Sticks and stones may break my bones, but names will never hurt me"[4] is completely erroneous. The words hurled at me were like a heavy chain that hung around my neck and

4 *The Christian Recorder*, March, 1862

inwardly bent me in two. They reminded me constantly of my failures and uselessness, and affirmed to me that I was absolutely worthless and positively unlovable.

I hated my life. I wished that I had never been born and that my eyes had never opened to the light of day; however, we have no control over these events. These choices belong only to God. He is the one who decides our day of birth and He alone knows the day of our death. He also chooses the womb in which we will be nurtured, our families of origin, and the places where we will grow up. My question for many years was, *Why this family, and why these parents?*

Writing a book about one's life is very difficult when you have twelve siblings. Out of the thirteen of us, ten seemed to be treated, for the most part, as valued members of the family. Years later some of my younger brothers told me that after I left home, they occasionally were subjected to abuse. However, the three of us (Cynthia, Joseph and I) were treated as misfits and outcasts the entire time we lived at home. My story is very much intertwined with that of the other misfits, and periodically I cannot help but reveal parts of their stories. However, I have done my very best to protect them and respect their privacy.

While I was writing the first draft of this book, my sister Cynthia, died at the age of sixty-six of a heart attack, and I was asked by her daughter to deliver her eulogy. I was deeply moved to be given this opportunity to honour her, as I loved my sister Cynthia very much. Although we lived in different provinces, we made a point of talking on the phone every other week. Her death hit me hard because I know for a fact that she had not been able to work her way through the countless issues resulting from her childhood abuse. I suspected her childhood stress had negatively affected her health over the years. After her death, her husband of forty years told me that he had never understood why the three of us were treated differently from the other siblings. I was surprised that he knew about our secret history as he had never referred to it. He quietly conveyed to me that he observed that we were at times treated shamefully, but he felt as an outsider he could never intervene. When he talked to Cynthia about it, she would cover it over or make excuses for their behaviour.

In spite of the events of her childhood, Cynthia grew up to become a truly wonderful person. She was the essence of compassion, generous to a fault, a very caring sibling, an authentic friend, a responsible employee, a faithful wife, a loving mother, a doting grandmother and a dedicated volunteer in her community. My brother Joseph also grew up to become a loving husband and an outstanding father. He has also been a tremendous influence on others in the many communities in which he has lived.

You may ask yourself, *Why did he write this book? Couldn't he just walk away from the past and let it go? Couldn't he just leave it behind?* If only it were that simple! About twenty-five years ago I began the struggle to be liberated from my past, as it was disrupting my present and I knew it would destroy my future. I also knew if I did not deal with it, it would haunt me forever, and I feared that I would eventually end up in an institution amongst those who suffer terminal breakdowns. Choosing to face the past and move into the future relatively whole is not for the faint of heart. The healing process is extremely difficult; at times, when going through it, it feels like being operated on without anesthesia. Many people who have been treated unjustly live in denial and consequently live unfulfilled lives. They remain prisoners in the chains that have been forged for them by others. Not only are the victims in prison, but their abusers or the witnesses of the abuse are also imprisoned. I long to unlock the prison doors and declare to them and to the world that they can be completely liberated; they no longer need to bury the pain, the guilt, or the shame of what they suffered or did or witnessed.

Please believe me when I tell you that this book is not written in a spirit of malice or condemnation. In my heart, soul, mind and spirit I have experienced a tremendous healing process and I am free. I write to help others become free from the physical, mental, verbal, emotional, sexual and spiritual shackles that linger. Horrid memories can haunt, sometimes on a daily basis, thirty, forty or even sixty years after the events occurred. Remembrance, or what I call *feeling memories*, can be brought on by a smell, a word, or a sudden flashback; when this occurs, one can feel powerless to stop the invasion. The recollections themselves are in our memory bank, and although we may have received healing and therapy to remove the pain and stingers, the memories remain. They are part of our history, and we cannot change that history by whitewashing or burying it.

Our stories are part of who we are today, and in order to live in the liberty and freedom we are meant to enjoy, we have to truthfully and courageously face our past. Although the past can be healed, no one can magically change the past or erase what has happened to us. I know these things, because I did not want to face my past, but I also knew it was holding me hostage. It would not permit me to move into the future and live my life as a whole human being.

Please know that it was never my original intention to tell my story openly. There are three reasons why I hesitated for so long. First, I knew that if I were to tell my story I have to go back to the abyss or to the basement of my soul, look once again at the hurts and stir up the memories that were part of my history. I knew in writing my story that I could not nullify the raw emotions that would naturally come to the surface of such remembering. Second, I had no desire to cause alienation or pain for my siblings and extended family members. If they *choose* to read this book, they need to remember that this is *my* story and not theirs. At one time I even considered writing this book under a pseudonym, but for me that seemed dishonest and I strive to be a person of honesty and integrity. The third reason I hesitated so long is that I am in a very public profession and was not sure I wanted to take the risk of exposing myself in such a vulnerable way. What would others think of such a story and how would they receive it? Would I be judged and ostracized? Only time will tell, but for the sake of those who have been wounded, I have decided to risk it. Although I have spoken freely in the public square for over thirty years, it has only been in the past two years that I have spoken about forgiveness and healing of childhood sufferings in congregational settings. When I have done so, others have told me that they felt encouraged, validated and open to discuss similar sufferings that they went through. Some have commented: "It's wonderful to know that I am not alone." Many have urged me to write my story because others deserve to know that, indeed, they are not alone in the suffering and abuses they have also endured. In my sixty-plus years, I have heard stories of horrible childhoods, violent multiple marriages, drug, alcohol, sex and pornography addictions that are used in an attempt to hide or dull the constant pain people live in. Sadly, all too often many of them repeat the same history and take out their frustrations and anger on the ones they are called to love. Far too many have wandered through life filled with guilt and shame, wondering if anyone could possibly ever love them. Others are terrified to speak of their upbringing, for they fear that the ghosts of the past still have the power to abuse and torture them. Some will not speak of the abuse they endured as children as they fear they are being unfaithful to the dead or they are not honouring their father and mother. But truth does not dishonour those who have predeceased us; truth always sets people free. Others are so filled with guilt and shame that they dare not speak because they fear they may start weeping and may never be able to stop. There have been many times when I have wept for days on end, but eventually the tears stop and I have been able to move forward with courage and grace.

I want all those who are reading this book to know that deliverance from evil is possible. This book is about that deliverance and new life. New life came to me and it can certainly come to you!

CHAPTER ONE
Through The Eyes Of Others

"Ronnie, Ronnie, Ronnie. Ronnie—
come and clean up this mess."
"Ronnie, come and hang up these coats."
"Ronnie, come and pick up my pencil."
"Ronnie, come and tie my skates."
"Ronnie, the bathroom is dirty."
"Ronnie, you didn't change the sheets on my bed."
"Ronnie, come and rock the baby!"
"Ronnie! Ronnie! Ronnie!"

Early on in my life, I learned to hate that name. *Ronnie, do this!* they'd demand, and *Ronnie do that!* Whenever I was called, I recoiled inside. Even today, when people call me Ronnie, I have an automatic reaction deep in my soul. Consequently, when I introduce myself it is always *Ron*, or, if it's in a more formal setting (such as a doctor's or dentist's office), it is *Ronald.*

In the prologue, I told you what my parents were like. So, in turn, it's only fair to ask: What was *I* like as a child? At times, we may look at ourselves through rose-coloured glasses, and truthfully most of us can't remember the finer details of who we were as children. Twenty-five years ago, when I began to unpack my past, I wrote to five of my siblings who were closest in age to me, asking them what they remembered about me as a child. At the time I wrote I was thirty-nine years old and my life was a mess. I was looking for answers. I was desperate and I needed to know who I was.

Four of my siblings responded and similar threads ran through their letters: Cynthia told me that she could not find it within herself to respond; Joseph responded briefly as the memories were still too painful for him. Three siblings remembered me as a quiet kid full of self-confidence when *away* from home, but they noted that I was different at home. There, they wrote, I stayed in the background, not wanting to draw attention to myself. I learned early on not to cry or show that I was hurt, either emotionally or physically. One sister told me my older brother was a problem child and that I had been told to keep an eye on him. That job ended with both of us becoming the family outcasts. Joseph may have been perceived as a problem child because during his first year, he did not live with the rest of the family. Immediately after he was born he was sent to live with Nana, my maternal grandmother. His older siblings had been diagnosed with some kind of contagious childhood sickness and he could not be exposed to the other children, for his protection. He became Nana's favourite grandchild and never bonded with my mother. Again, this may be family folklore, but it is what we were told.

My five siblings all reacted in the same manner to my probing questions about our past. I had put them all in an uncomfortable position, and although most of them responded, I believe they did so reluctantly. I kept their letters in my healing file. I told them that I was going through a major crisis and I desperately needed their help. Today, I remain very grateful; they helped me work through the process of healing. I basically wanted to know if I had been a rebellious child, therefore deserving at least some of the severe punishment I received. It was helpful for me to know that in spite of what was taking place in our home, I was more or less a normal child. After going through my healing process I have come to the conclusion that many in my family continue to suffer from survivor's guilt as they escaped the brunt of the terrible abuse that the three of us endured. In this instance, survivor's guilt can be summed up by saying that the others carry guilt, blaming themselves for not being able to rescue those being abused.

One sister wrote, *I must honestly say that I have tried to put my youth behind me. I see my days then and my life now as lives led by two different people, but I understand how the demons can creep up on you.* It was this sister who realized that the children who were not abused had a tenuous hold on their positions in the family, which could have changed in the twinkling of an eye. Another sister said that in order to escape the violence and pain going on around her she became engrossed in books. She also confessed that out of fear she did not want to dig too deep into our lives as children: *Every now and again things surface that bring back pain and anger I don't understand, but not enough to make me truly dig up the bones and examine them. I suppose I should delve into this, but I don't think it is worth it for me. I may not be a whole person on this earth, but I expect a full healing in heaven.*

A letter from one of my brothers was almost an apology for the role that he played in some of the abuse that was carried out daily against my older brother and me. When Joseph responded, he wrote, *Ron, you and I both know there are some places in life it is hard to visit, and sometimes we intentionally stay away from those places and that statement is very true for me. I no longer visit there, and I don't want to go there, at least not at this time in my life. I don't even want to remember if I remember.*

Another sibling wrote, *Over the years I've thought hundreds of times of how we treated you, and how we were allowed to treat you, and I cringe . . . in my mind I've apologized a million times to the three of you, but it is a dark spot on my soul, and I can't take it back.*

Another wrote, *I remember, as I got a little older, about you and Joseph being treated differently. I don't think of that part of my life that much. I feel ashamed about my behaviour during that time . . . I remember that you and Joseph were forced to wear old, ragged clothes at home. I remember that you often wore running shoes that had to be tied on your feet by string. It makes me very sad to think about these things, and I can only say I'm sorry that I did not speak up for you then.*

If any of my siblings choose to read this book, I want them to know that I do not in any way hold them the least bit responsible for the abuse that they witnessed or participated in. They were children walking on eggshells and did not have a choice, or else they too would have become victims of horrific abuse. I think all my siblings grew up with the knowledge that, in a moment, in the twinkling of an eye, things could change and they too could end up wearing rags or girl's dresses and waiting hand and foot on the others. It was my mother who made Joseph and me slaves for our siblings and herself, and it is she who bears the full responsibility for these actions. My father, of course, bears some of the responsibility as he could not help but be aware of this behaviour, yet he did nothing to intervene.

Why me? To this day, I do not know. All I know is that I was very, very young when the abuse began and that it started completely out of the blue. I do, however, have this memory: I must have been three or four years old, and my mother, whom I loved dearly at that time, was feeding one of my baby brothers. As she spoon-fed the baby his porridge, she made me stand at attention in front of her. She must have been annoyed with me and told me to stand in front of her and not to move. Then she took a spoonful of hot porridge and threw it in my eye and told me that now my eye would fall out. Even as a three- or four-year-old child, I knew in an instant that I was standing in the presence of something very evil. I knew at that moment something demonic was taking place, although I could not express this in words. All I could do was stand there with the porridge running down my face, silently praying that my eye would be fine. While I was praying my fear evaporated. I knew that something evil had happened, but I also knew that there was something more powerful that could and would protect me.

Another time I was told to pick up the toys that one of my baby brothers had thrown out of the playpen. While I was down on my hands and knees gathering them up, my brother in the playpen hit me on the head with his toy drum. He was not trying to hurt me, but he cut my head and it started bleeding profusely. I thought I was bleeding to death, and I was frightened and started to cry. Instead of comforting me, my mother kicked me repeatedly as I lay bleeding on the floor. She was angry and I felt that I was responsible for the blood on the floor. I couldn't understand why I was being punished for something beyond my control.

Almost sixty years later, these two episodes are still etched on my soul and very much alive in my memory bank. To this day I recall the pain of the hot porridge hitting my eye and the drum pounding on my head.

After that it just got worse. I believe that the constant abuse began because I came to my older brother Joseph's defence. I do not think I am a particularly brave person, but perhaps as a child I had far less fear. I remember that my brother had to make all the beds and do all the housecleaning before going to school. I did not think that was fair. When bad things happen in our lives, a child thinks there must be a reason. A child needs an adult to explain why one child is treated unfairly. When I spoke up in defence of Joseph, I was punished by having to share his chores. At first, I had to clean all the baseboards in the house every morning. This was not an onerous task and I was delighted to help him. However, querying his persecution put me directly in the cross fire of my mother's anger. My questions about the unfairness of the situation led me down a path of suffering that haunted me until I finally left home at the age of twenty.

Reflecting on my childhood, I cannot think of anything but the pain. Yes, I know there must have been happy times, but if there were, I remember very few. I have tried to remember good times or safe times, but I think the abuse overwhelms any good times I may have enjoyed. I recall constantly walking as if on eggshells, of being continually on guard. Looking back, I see myself perpetually staying in the shadows while attempting to be a really good boy. Recently there has been a focus in Canada concerning Post Traumatic Stress Disorder, and hypervigilance is one symptom of PTSD. When you have to be vigilant at all times, you grow anxious and anxiety leads to exhaustion. In the environment in which I was raised I had to be wise beyond my years when trying to measure the emotional temperature the moment I entered the house. I always wondered when or why the next unexpected blow might land, the next meal would be denied, or the next beating inflicted. Therefore I lived in a state of constant fear. I was fearful of what the day would bring when I got up in the morning, fearful that I might not be able to go to school, fearful that I would be late for school, fearful when I came home from school, fearful that I would not have time to do my homework, fearful that I would unknowingly do something wrong, fearful that I would not be fed, fearful when I went to bed. I was fearful again when I got up the next morning and the cycle would continue. Fear was my close companion, and there were many times I wished that I had never been born. When I went to bed at night and prayed that well-known children's bedtime prayer, "Now I Lay Me Down to Sleep," I meant it when I prayed, *If I should die before I wake, I pray the Lord my soul to take.* For most of my childhood, I regretted waking up each morning. I was so disappointed that He had not taken me during the night, but I thought that God couldn't take me because I was evil and unlovable.

Looking back, I remember only two joyful occasions from my childhood:

The family was going on vacation to Prince Edward Island, but we three misfits were not permitted to go. To us it was a joy, because everyone else in the family was gone and we were home by ourselves. For two whole weeks it was like paradise. While the family was away, my paternal grandmother came to stay with us. Gra, as we called her, was wonderful, and we thought she was very holy as she constantly prayed the Rosary. She wore braces on her legs because she had severe arthritis. Her days with us were the most joy-filled two weeks of my childhood. We were outside every day, running carefree through the fields, eating wonderful meals at the table on normal plates and playing games from early in the morning to late at night. We never went to bed hungry. Every night, Gra would put out a plate of cookies she had made and the four of us would play cards. During that blissful time I did not care if my family ever returned to Sydney. I would have been content to live with Gra for the rest of my life, but it was not going to happen. Eventually the family came back and things returned to normal. Although she didn't know it, my grandmother played a major role in my life. I will share later in this book how her influence profoundly impacted me.

The second joyful occasion I remember was my first day of school in Sydney, Nova Scotia. When we were posted to Sydney, we lived for a time in Sydney Pier, and the military provided a van for us to travel to the Air Force Base for school. I remember I was sitting in the back of the van between my siblings when the bus driver was told that it was my first day of school. He came to the back of the van and reached down, picked me up in his arms, and carried me to the front seat of the van to sit beside him. Why is this memory so etched in my mind? It may seem silly, but it was the only time in my childhood that I remember being held affectionately. I remember the fleeting seconds it took him to carry me from the back seat of the van to the front, and how good it felt having someone hold me gently in their arms. I felt warm, loved, and wanted, and that memory remains a precious gift to me sixty years later.

CHAPTER TWO
School

"No, you are not going to school today. You will stay home and clean. I don't care if it's Valentine's, Halloween, Christmas or a school trip. You are not going, and don't bother asking me again!"

I absolutely loved going to school, because it was an escape from staying at home. If I stayed home, I knew that I would endure a day of beating and abuse, so I would do everything in my power to attend school. But after we moved from Sydney Pier to the Air Force base, school became a tremendous hardship for my brother and me. From grades one to six, until we left Sydney for Ottawa, my mother ordered Joseph and me to stand on the back step of the school during recess and playtime and face our house across the field; we were forbidden to play. Day after day from, September to June—for six years—we stood at the back of the school facing our house so Mother could keep an eye on us from the house and make sure we did not disobey her.

I still cannot understand why the principal or any of the teachers did not ask us why we were standing there while everyone else was playing. No one ever came out and questioned us or encouraged us to go and play. For six full years, approximately eighteen hundred school days, for a twenty-minute recess in the morning and a twenty-minute recess in the afternoon, we stood on the back steps of that school. When you add up all that time, we stood there for almost two thousand hours—and to this child, it seemed as if no one noticed.

No, I refuse to believe that so many were blind to what was happening. Because of their non-intervention, I felt that they were participants in the abuse. Elie Wiesel in his acceptance speech of his Nobel Peace Prize in 1986 said:

> "Whenever and wherever human beings endure suffering and humiliation, we must always take sides. Neutrality helps the oppressor, never the victim. Silence encourages the tormentor, never the tormented. Sometimes we must interfere. When human lives are endangered, when human dignity is in jeopardy, national borders and sensitivities become irrelevant."[5]

Those who witnessed these and other events may have been intimidated by my parents' position in the community and felt that if they became involved it would come back on them. If anyone dared to ask, we could never tell why we were standing on the steps or why we had bruises and marks on our arms and legs, or why we didn't play with others; family loyalty reigned supreme in our home. The opinion of our neighbours and those in our community was more important than what was

5 https://www.nobelprize.org/nobel_prizes/peace/laureates/1986/wiesel-acceptance_en.html

happening behind closed doors. In our house, the rules were: do not feel, do not trust, and, whatever you do, do not tell. As a result, we would never reveal to others what was going on in our home or why we never left the steps to play. If we moved off the step or even sat down on the steps, we would have no lunch when we went home at noon—or we would be severely beaten the moment we walked through the door. Even in winter, when recesses were cancelled, we didn't dare stay inside and play with the other children. No, we had to go outside, and if we didn't, we would be punished. On the days that the wind and snow were fully directed at the spot where we stood, we were not allowed to move. We could not even go around the corner for shelter and stick our heads out so that Mother would know we were there and not disobeying her by playing. No, we stood there and froze. When I was a child, I did not understand how she could know when we were not on the back step. It was not until I was fifty that the penny finally dropped.

My wife and I and my two best friends travelled to Sydney in 2001. I had not been back since I was a child. The house we had lived in was still standing. I stood on the steps of that house and looked across at the school, and at last I understood. The school stood in a quadrangle of backyards; no trees or other buildings obstructed the view of it from the house. The distance from my house to the school was much shorter than I had remembered as a child. All my mother had to do was stand at the window and look out and she could see us clearly. I finally realized how she always knew when I dared move off that step. At long last, I understood why I would get to class every single day one minute late as she made us wait until the very last minute before we could leave for school. Inevitably, the bell would ring when we were halfway across the field running at full speed to reach the school. Day after day we would walk into the classroom late and embarrassed. There were days when I could not stand it anymore and I would dash off the step and run and play with my classmates, knowing that when I arrived home, my punishment would be a missed lunch or a beating. At those times I simply didn't care. I ran with abandon as I wanted so much to be free. I wanted to experience the liberty of running with the wind in my face and the joy of playing like the other children. I wanted to know what it would be like to play with a friend. I wanted to know what it would be like to have a friend. I prayed that God would keep her from seeing me play. As a child, I didn't know how she knew when I was playing, but He never answered those prayers. Other days I missed school because I was not allowed to put my shoes on until the last minute, and when I would go to the back door to put them on, they were not there. My mother would hide them, and if I did not find them quickly enough, I would be too late to go to school. I would find them in the linen closet underneath the sheets and towels, or in the oven, or in some other strange place where shoes just did not belong. It was a cruel game, and I never knew what day she would choose to play it.

On that visit to Sydney in 2001, there was no response when I knocked on the door of our old house. I was tempted to leave a note asking if we could come back and wander through the house. But suddenly I was overwhelmed and could not wait to leave. The memories that flooded back as I stood on those steps brought so much terror that I panicked and ran back to the car and asked my friends to drive away as quickly as possible. How could fifty-year-old memories hold such torment and horror that a middle-aged man would want to flee in terror? Just before starting to write my story, I went up to Sydney one last time. The houses had been torn down and I thanked God, because for me that house was a house of horrors and evil and deserved to be reduced to rubble. We three children had been reduced to nothing while we lived under that roof.

Most evenings, we also had to clean the house; inevitably, that kept us from studying. As a consequence, we fell behind the other students. Not only did we do cleaning, we had to serve our siblings, too. If one dropped a pencil, I had to come and pick it up. If one wanted to put on a pair of socks or skates in the winter, one of us was called and we had to put them on our sibling's feet. My mother encouraged this behaviour in my siblings, but I firmly believe they were far too young to truly appreciate what was happening. It was when we had to serve our older brothers in the same fashion that resentment and anger grew in my heart.

As much as I cried out to God, He did not make it so I could go to school on Valentine's Day or Halloween, or be involved in Christmas pageants or other festive events. On such occasions my mother would tell the teachers that I was sick; then I would endure a day of completing difficult, dirty household chores under my mother's constant supervision, as well as severe discipline. I will never forget being selected by my teacher to play the Little Drummer Boy in the Christmas pageant. It was to be an evening event in front of the whole community. To my absolute astonishment, my mother gave permission for me to participate, so I practised constantly. I was so honoured to be able to play and to sing to Baby Jesus. But at the very last minute, when I had my clothes and boots on to leave the house, my mother forbade me to go. She made me stay home and I was absolutely heartbroken. My hopes had been built up so high, and then at the very last second, dashed to the ground. I remember going into my bedroom, closing the door, and beating myself on my chest, arms, legs and head because I was so bad that my mother made me stay home. I can't tell you how disappointed I was. Oh, the hatred that started growing in my heart! However, the one thing she could not do was to stop me from singing that song in my heart—and I continue to sing it sixty years later. It is one of my favourite Christmas carols, and my Christmas is not complete unless I hear it over and over again. I loved the song, because in grade one or two, I really wanted to give Baby Jesus something for Christmas, because as a line in the song says, "I am a poor boy too . . ." It wasn't physical poverty I was thinking about as a child, but poverty of affection and love. I was desperate to be held and to be loved. As a good Catholic boy, I wanted with all my heart to please Mother Mary, and hoped that after I played and sang to her Son, she would spare a second and hold me in her arms. My childhood opportunity to play my drum for Him was taken from me. Today, however, in my home and in my car during the Christmas season, I can sing the song out loud. In my mind and heart, I know that I am still that little boy playing his drum for Baby Jesus.

One particular day, when I was being punished and not allowed to go to school, my older sister Cynthia had been given permission to leave for school at the very last minute. She was running as fast as she could so she would not be late. She was halfway across the field to the school when the school bell rang. She stopped dead in her tracks in the middle of the field when she heard the bell and knew she would be late again. She turned around, looked back at the house and hurled all of her schoolbooks and papers up in the air in absolute frustration. As I stood and watched her, my mother was also watching, and my heart ached. I fully understood her desperation. My mother seemed to get such twisted satisfaction out of keeping the three of us at home after all the others had left for school, knowing full well we would be marked late every day. When we were late in those days, we had to stand up in class and tell everyone why we were late. So almost every day we went to school we were shamed in front of the whole class. Mother knew when the bell was just about to ring, and she would allow us to leave only seconds before. Although we ran as fast as our little legs would carry us, it was never fast enough to get us inside the school and behind our desks in time. As I sadly observed my sister's reaction in the middle of the field that day, my heart broke for her. I felt the hopelessness and powerlessness in her action as she threw her books in the air. It was as if she had finally given up. She knew that while she lived under our mother's control and abuse there was absolutely nothing she could do to change it or stop it.

My older brother, who endured even more abuse than I did, was my hero while we were growing up. He was so much braver than I. One day our mother was punishing him at lunch hour, and she knocked out two of his front teeth. She made him go back to school that afternoon, and told him when he returned home after school he was to tell our father that he had fallen on the way home. The only problem with this deceitful plan was that my father was already home when my brother arrived and he could not understand why there was no fresh blood. I am sure my father knew what had happened, but did not want to confront my mother and provoke her temper. I believe my father knew my mother had anger management problems, even though she was careful to keep it well hidden from him.

For a long time, I had thought Cynthia, Joseph, and I were the only victims of my mother's rages. However, some time ago, a younger brother told me that my mother, in a fit of rage, twisted his arm up behind his back until she broke it. He had to cover it up by telling people that he had fallen out of a tree. Once she took a pair of pliers and tried to twist off Joseph's fingernails. His fingers and his heart bear the scars of this torture to this day. Another time she took a hot iron and set it on his back, burning him very badly. On this occasion, Cynthia took responsibility for the incident as my mother promised that she would stop beating and torturing us if my sister said that she did it by accident. We naïvely thought that this would be the turning point in our childhood, but instead it was just another lie to cover up abuse that might come to the attention of anyone outside the family.

Although I said earlier I was not going to tell the stories of my siblings, I have given you a tiny glimpse into our shared life. I want to expose the environment in which we were raised. Again, this abuse was not limited to the three of us, because others in the family from time to time were also victims of my mother's rage. I know some of their stories. However, I would have to say that most of our mother's outbursts were directed at the three of us.

My brother Joseph and I were very close and I valued his companionship. When I was weeping or nursing sore hands and legs, he understood what it felt like and was the essence of compassion. We slept in the same bed for almost fifteen years, head to foot, and ate off the same plates and wore the same dirty rags around the house. We had a lot in common, but my brother was much braver than I. Joseph ran away, not just once, but time and time again. When I look back, it seemed as if he ran away every single year. He had the courage to run away; I wished I had the courage to go with him, but I did not. As much as I wanted to leave, I was the fearful one. When he ran away the first time, things in the house suddenly changed. The beatings stopped, the excessive punishment ceased, and Mother promised that she would never do the things she had done if only he would come back home. When he did return, the beatings resumed within a few days, and even more outrageous and excessive punishments were introduced to us. School, playtime, affection and love were withheld from us, and finally food was used as a weapon to torment us as well.

CHAPTER THREE
Daily Living

"You didn't complete the chores I gave you to do, so you are not having supper…you left the step today at school…so you are not having supper…you wet the bed last night, so you are not having supper…you didn't run home from school fast enough…and so you are not having supper. And the list goes on and on…but you are not having supper."

One of my mother's favourite methods of punishment was to deprive us of food. She used food both to torture and reward us. There were days when, if we did anything wrong or even looked at my mother the wrong way, we were deprived of a meal. Like prisoners of war, our focus became food. When we lived in Sydney, my brother and I were not allowed to eat at the table because my mother said we were not fit to do so. We had to stand at the end of the kitchen counter and eat after everyone else had finished their meal. Our plates, cups and cutlery were different from those of the rest of the family. These were washed and then stored separately after all the other dishes had been put away. Our siblings were told that Joseph and I were poison and that our plates were toxic. There was never any danger of any of them using our plates. After my brother had run away from home once again, our mother took those toxic dishes, cups and cutlery and put them in a bottom drawer in the kitchen. She promised fervently that they would never be used again. If I had been smarter or braver, I would have taken them and broken them into tiny pieces. A few days after my brother returned, the dishes were taken from the drawer and once again put into use.

When everyone had left the kitchen, my brother and I would quickly eat our dinner and then wolf down any leftovers on our siblings' plates. If we were not quick enough and the food had been thrown into the garbage, we retrieved it and ate it. On numerous occasions, I took chicken bones out of the garbage and sucked out the marrow to try to fill the emptiness in my stomach. As a teenager I was constantly hungry, going to bed hungry and waking up hungry. I once went into a grocery store in Ottawa and stole food—not sweets or pop, but a package of bologna, because I desperately craved something to fill that void within me. I knew that I was not only hungry for food but for love and a sense of belonging. I felt absolutely empty.

Joseph and I eventually stole food out of the cupboards or the fridge, but we made a point of always sharing it with each other. From time to time we would get into the freezer and steal a loaf of bread or a jelly roll, but eventually my mother put a lock on the freezer. On nights when we didn't get supper, Joseph would sneak down to the kitchen in the middle of the night to get some food so we could have something in our stomachs. But eventually we got caught and the punishment at times was more than I could bear.

There was one punishment that happened only once, but I have never forgotten how frightened I was: In our Sydney home, there were two trap doors underneath the house—one facing north and the other south. When I was about eight or ten, my mother told my brother and me that because we stole food and were so bad we would have to go to reform school. We didn't know what that meant, but were told we deserved this punishment. But instead of being sent to reform school, which would bring shame on the family, we were each made to climb down through the trapdoors, which led to a crawl space underneath the house. We were told we were going to spend the rest of our lives living under the house; that would be our punishment and our new home. It was a frightening place, with only a gravel floor and lots of creepy bugs. Down there, in the pitch black, I was petrified that I would never see the light of day again. No blankets, no food, no companionship—just darkness! (To this day, I don't like enclosed spaces or rooms that are completely dark.) I did not understand what made me or my brother so bad that we deserved such harsh punishment. As far as I was concerned, this shouldn't even have been done to an animal.

We were probably down under the house for four or five hours. One of my older brothers, the family favourite, came home later that evening and discovered what my parents had done. He was furious and demanded that we be removed from underneath the house. I do not know if it was because he shamed my parents into releasing us, or because he was a favourite son, but whatever the case he was able to get what he wanted. All I know is, that night my brother was our deliverer. That day he did not rescue a poor frightened little boy, but rather an *absolutely terrified* little boy. I will never forget that he rescued me and Joseph. Whatever he said to my parents was effective; they did not repeat that punishment ever again.

Another abusive practice was to constantly shame us. When we came home from school we had to change into our cleaning clothes. That is what they were called, but they weren't even clothes—they were rags. The pants and shirts we wore were full of holes like Swiss cheese, and hung like rags on our backs. We wore cast-off running shoes that had to be tied to our feet with string to stay on. Every now and then, my mother made my brother wear a dress around the house while he cleaned. Could she heighten his shame any further? From the time we got home from school until we went to bed, all we did was clean. Consequently, my brother failed grade six and I eventually failed grade nine. At that time I desperately needed glasses, but I didn't dare tell my parents because I felt I would be blamed for my weak eyes. That might sound laughable, but as a child, I felt everything was my fault. I needed glasses, and so I stole a pair from a student in my class who wore them only occasionally. They did not improve my vision, and I failed that year of school.

During summer holidays the punishments were unique in themselves. Oh, how I hated school to end! While I went to school I was free from the monster for five or six hours a day, but when summer came, my life became hell. In Sydney there was a break during the blueberry-picking season. Every morning we went to pick blueberries to sell to help pay the household expenses. I enjoyed this as it enabled me to be outdoors and have some fun out in nature. But in the afternoons, I cleaned house or sat on the back step and watched my siblings play until just before my father came home from work. Like clockwork my father came in the door at 4:30 every day. At 4:25 my mother would allow me to leave the step to go and play. At 4:35 she would call me in from outside and say, "You have been out playing all day, now come in and do some chores." I had to go along with the charade, because if I didn't there would be no supper, and the next day after my father left for work, I would be severely beaten.

Joseph was still at home while we lived in Sydney, and if I was fortunate enough to have supper, my mother would then pull me aside and tell me to go to bed—at 5:30 in the evening! This wasn't a punishment for Joseph as one of us had to be around to clean or wait on our siblings. Every night of the year I was in bed by 5:30, and all I could do was lie there and listen to the sounds of my brothers and sisters and their friends playing outside my bedroom window. In the summer it was baseball and in the winter it was ice hockey. While they were all playing, my childhood was wasting away, and there was not a thing I could do about it. I was an outcast and not permitted to be part of the family evening playtime. I was not allowed to do anything in bed and my mother would come sneaking down the hall to make sure that no one was keeping me company or that I was not hiding under the covers reading a book. What would I do in bed? I would beat myself; I would beat my arms, legs, and chest with my fists to punish myself for being bad. I believed it was my fault that I was being punished so severely. I figured I must be evil and that evil people should be punished. I suppose if I had had access to a razor blade or a needle I would have cut or pierced myself in an attempt to release the evil from my body. I often hoped that one day they would find me dead in bed. I fantasized that if the family wanted to know why I died, the doctor would say, "Why do you think he died? He died of a broken heart and loneliness."

The only time I felt that anyone understood was one winter evening when my sister Cynthia was walking by my room. She heard me sobbing into my mattress (Joseph and I were not permitted pillows), so she came in and asked me what was wrong. At that moment it was the awful loneliness, but I could not explain it, so I said, "I don't know." Eventually, I stopped crying. And when I did, I heard my sister sobbing her heart out in her room across the hall from mine. I crept out of bed and sneaked across and asked her why she was crying. She responded as I had earlier: "I don't know." Even though she also didn't know why either of us were crying, I have never forgotten her compassion and empathy for my lonely and broken heart.

When we moved to Ottawa, there were no more blueberry picking days, and so two new forms of punishment robbed me of any joy as a child. Every day of summer, my mother would dream up a cleaning project or some other work-related task. From 8:00 in the morning until 4:20 in the evening I would be assigned a particular job. One year it was untangling a fishing line that was rolled in a ball that was impossible to untangle. I had to sit on the stairs for eight hours a day and try to untangle that impossible mess. A second task was to take the pots, roasting pans, cake pans and cookie sheets and scrub them until they looked like new. I would spend eight hours a day on my knees at the top of the basement stairs so she could watch me from the kitchen as I scrubbed the pots and pans. When I thought I was finished I would have to start over again, and so there never was an end. For those eight hours I was not allowed to move from that spot. At 4:20 she would tell me to clean up and go outside and play. At 4:30 my father came home from work, and once again at 4:35 I would be called into the house.

I use words to make a living, but there are no words that can adequately describe those days. They were the loneliest and longest days of my young life. I wish I could share with you the tears I shed. At times, I cried so hard I thought my heart would break in two. I ached to be outside playing. I ached for someone to hold me and tell me that life was more than I was experiencing. During those long hours in bed or on the stairs, untangling fishing line or scrubbing pots and pans, I felt a total sense of abandonment. I felt as if the world had ended and I was the only one left behind. On those days, again and again, I cried out to God to come and rescue me and take me out of this awful, evil house. But it was as though the heavens were brass and my prayers fell uselessly to the ground.

An abused child will think that this is what life is all about. Such a child thinks they are trapped in this existence forever. They have no concept of time and therefore don't realize that one day they will grow up and leave home. No, they believe that home, where beatings and cruelty run rampant, is all there is in this life. An abused child grows up not trusting, not feeling, and not telling. After all, who would ever believe that a good God-fearing Catholic family, in church every week, would have so many sinister and foreboding secrets behind closed doors?

When I was about five or six years old, my eldest brother lost the watch my parents had given him as a gift. My mother immediately blamed me and accused me of stealing the watch. I had to search the house for the watch I had allegedly stolen. I had not even seen the watch and I did not know what it looked like. I had not stolen it and had no idea what I was looking for or where to begin, so my mother began to beat me. I know if someone is beaten long enough and hard enough they will confess to absolutely anything. They will confess to whatever their tormentor wants. After about an hour of beating I finally confessed to this imaginary theft. My mother had beaten the backs of my hands with a toilet plunger until they were swollen to twice their normal size. I had to put them in ice water to bring the swelling down before my father got home. When my father arrived, my mother told him that I had confessed to stealing the watch, that I had smashed it and thrown away the pieces, so he beat me again. He was not stupid. He was a military policeman and he could see my swollen hands, but that did not seem to alert him. At that time, I naïvely thought my father did not really know what was going on in our house. But after he whipped me that day, I realized that he would never intervene on my behalf.

On that day, I lost part of my innocence. I had always thought that if you told the truth, you would not be punished. I was six or seven years old and I began to realize that I lived in an environment that was not safe. Regardless of whether I was innocent or guilty, it was enough for someone to think that I was responsible for whatever had happened. From that time onward, if anything in the house was missing, I was blamed and would be beaten until I confessed. So over time I did become a thief and a liar. I learned to lie and to steal, especially food, but I did it in order to survive and in an attempt to fill my inner emptiness.

In 1966, when we moved to Ottawa, I had a new advantage: the school was not right across the field from our house. I had to take a bus to get to school and thought that now I would be able to play. But no, my mother was having none of that. She bought the whitest pair of pants she could find for me to wear to school every day. If I got them dirty or stained in any way, I would be thrashed when I got home. She encouraged my little brothers to keep an eye on me and they dutifully reported any transgression.

My sister Cynthia and brother Joseph were getting older, and around the time we moved to Ottawa, it was clear that they would soon be leaving home. My sister was five years my senior and my brother three years older. Eventually Cynthia left home to get married, and my brother Joseph left to take a job in Northern Ontario. I was now the last of the three abused children still living at home. With my two siblings gone, I was truly alone.

CHAPTER FOUR
All Alone

"Ronnie, you are absolutely useless! You are a runt and a failure. You're good for nothing; you're stupid and you will never amount to anything . . ."

With my sister Cynthia and my brother Joseph gone, I was now responsible for cleaning the entire house. I had known for years that this would happen, but when it became a reality, I entered into a new nightmare. The only thing I was forbidden to do was the dishes; I was still considered poison, so I was not allowed near the kitchen, except to scrub the floor and empty the garbage. My mother feared that I might find a way to steal food and satisfy my constant hunger. With my older brother no longer living at home, I finally had a bed to myself. For fifteen years I had slept with him. Now I was alone in the bed and it felt so empty. We had slept head to foot, and now the comfort of my brother's feet beside my head was gone.

Was it possible for my situation to get any worse? Unfortunately, yes, it did get much worse. Instead of three punching bags in the house, Mother now had only one, and I was her daily target. Her acts of violence and evil increased, or perhaps it just felt that way to me because I was alone. I could tell many horror stories, but I will limit myself to those that are most prominent in my mind.

One of the most important events in a person's life is their birthday, and, as such, many celebrate the anniversary of when we arrived in this world. Joseph's birthday was in January, and I was born in February. On the rare occasions our birthdays were acknowledged, they were celebrated together, but seldom with a cake and never with presents. I was never told the date of my birthday, although I was told it was in February. I decided to trick one of my sisters by telling her that I was born on the most important day in February—the 14th. She was quite upset that I would declare Valentine's Day my birthday, so she sought out my birth certificate, and I finally knew that February 7th was the day I was born. I was fourteen years old when I made this discovery. I cannot express the joy I felt in finally knowing the date of my birth. I was a complete person, not a piece of garbage, nor was I worthless, a runt, stupid, dumb, good-for-nothing, or any of the other degrading names that I was called in an attempt to destroy me mentally, physically, and emotionally.

When I started grade eleven, I felt betrayed even by my school. The school population had grown so large that half the students attended in the morning and half in the afternoon. I had to go from 7:00 a.m. until 12:30 p.m., and my brothers went in the afternoon. Thus I was home every afternoon. By that time, my older brothers and sisters who were married began having babies and my mother was paid to take care of these little ones. It didn't take long for me to become the chief babysitter, bottle washer, and diaper changer, in addition to all the regular housework I was required to do.

However, I discovered during this process that I loved children. I fed these little ones, bathed them, played with them, and loved them—and they loved me back. They didn't mock me for the filthy clothes I was forced to wear. Their love for me was unconditional, and in return I loved them unconditionally. I thanked God for these small graces in the midst of abusive chaos. With all the housework and caring for my nephews, my schoolwork suffered, but I learned a trick that enabled me to successfully pass my grades. As I went about doing my work, I memorized the school lessons so I would not have to repeat another grade. This was not because I was extremely clever, but because I was desperate; I could not spend one more day than necessary in that house. If I could manage to use what we had been taught in the classroom in tests and exams, I would pass—and it worked!

During my time babysitting, one incident stands out: Every day, when I walked in the door, I would be beaten. My mother would be waiting there for me inside the door with a weapon—the plunger, the dog's chain, a hockey stick, a belt, her heavy shoe with the wooden heel, even her bare hands. All I could do on the way home from school was worry about what I could have done wrong that day or which of my tasks would not measure up to her scrutiny. If I responded to those beatings in what my mother perceived to be a belligerent manner, she would wash my mouth out with lye soap, or fill my mouth with cayenne pepper or chili powder and force me to swallow it. One day my mother shoved a feces-filled diaper into my face. It went into my mouth, eyes, and nose. That appalling incident has never left my memory. I could handle the beatings, and if I cried and howled long enough, or if she drew sufficient blood, she would stop, but this dirty diaper incident finally broke my spirit. I remember it vividly to this day. While it was happening, everything seemed to be moving in slow motion, and I seemed to separate myself from my body. It was as though I was splitting into little pieces and losing a part of myself. I think it was on this day that whatever innocence I had left completely vanished. I realized that my mother had tipped over the edge. She was pushing me into an abyss out of which I would never escape. With that dirty diaper plastered all over my face, something inside me shattered. As I lay in a heap on the floor, all I could think was, *This is the woman who gave birth to me; why is she treating me like this? What did I ever do to deserve this kind of abuse?* I didn't understand what had just happened to me. Still on the floor, I thought, *This is the straw that has finally broken my back; I should flee from this house and never return.*

But I had no place to go. I could not go to a teacher, a priest, the police, or any other authority figure. When Joseph ran away once, he went to our parish priest; the priest called my parents, and they came and fetched Joseph. On the following Sunday, the priest preached a sermon on obeying your father and your mother. What an open-handed slap in the face for my brother, who had reached out to him for compassion and understanding. Recalling this, I knew I was trapped and could not get out unless I took my own life. I was just finishing grade eleven and I knew that I must at least finish grade twelve if I hoped to find any kind of employment. I wondered if I was a coward—or did it take more courage to remain in that toxic environment? To this day, I sometimes lie in bed at night and wonder how different my life would have been if I had chosen that day to run and never return, but I was far too afraid.

The abuse did something to my soul. I learned to lie, and I learned to steal food just to survive, but most of all I learned to hate. My mother taught me to hate her—and to mistrust my father with the familiar refrain, "Just wait until your father gets home." There was a time in my life when I was not permitted to call her *Mother* or *Mommy*. If I wanted to speak to her, I would come into the room and stand until she acknowledged my presence and asked me what I wanted. When I talked to my siblings I always referred to my mother as *her* or *she*. And so I became more withdrawn and more removed from those around me, and even from myself.

I despised all the festive occasions of the year. At Christmas, every corner of the house would be decorated, and under the tree there would be piles and piles of presents. Every year my presents would consist of clothes, a pair of white pants, and a shirt or a sweater. This is what I would wear to school for the next twelve months. My siblings would get clothes, toys, puzzles, games, skates, hockey sticks, and whatever else was on their wish list. If I did receive a toy or a game, it would be taken from me on Boxing Day and given to one of my siblings. At Easter, when my siblings were out looking for eggs, I was inside doing housework. At Halloween, my brothers and sisters went door to door and returned home with pillowcases filled with sweets, while I would be in my bed sobbing my heart out, missing yet another event. On their birthdays, it was always cake and presents. So not only did I learn to hate the holidays, I learned to hate my siblings.

At night, I would lie in bed and fantasize that someone would come and rescue me. Someone would come and tell me that I had been adopted into this hellhole and that the error had finally been discovered; I would be moved to a family who would love me. I wondered if there were families in the world that loved their children, or did this kind of abuse happen in every home? I fantasized that my parents had been killed and that all of us would be split up to live with different families; mine would be a home of love and tenderness. In my dream home, there would be no more plungers, no cords for whipping, no belts, no sticks, no dirty diapers, and no shoes with wooden heels. No longer would I hear words like *runt*, *worthless*, *stupid*, and *dumb*, along with *four eyes* and *good for nothing*.

For me, the worst day of the week was Sunday. As a good Catholic family, we did not dare miss attending Mass. When church was over my mother restricted me to the garage for the afternoon. What was my ridiculous job in the garage? One thing you can count on in a large family, week after week, is plenty of garbage. Every Sunday my mother would dump all the garbage out of the bags into a big pile on the garage floor. My task was to sort it and re-bag it for the garbage men to pick up. Not that my mother was ahead of her time and doing her best for the environment; this was a distorted punishment dreamed up to keep me from doing my homework or spending any time in the house on Sunday afternoons. In the summer the garbage was full of maggots, and in the winter I would spend hours in the garage, shivering in my cleaning clothes with my hands, legs, and feet freezing. If there had been seven bags of garbage, I had to reduce this to three or four. After a time, I got quite good at doing this. However, if I completed the job too quickly, all the bags were once again emptied on the floor by my mother and I would have to repeat the process. If I protested or cried, I was beaten with whatever tool or instrument was available in the garage. It is excruciatingly painful for a child to be beaten on the arms, hands, and legs with a hockey stick, especially when freezing cold. And so I grew to hate Sundays. I felt unwanted, unworthy, and completely unloved, and I was garbage. Ron the garbage man! Ron, the slave! Ron, make bricks without straw!

Did I hate my parents? Yes! At times I hated them with all my heart. I lived with my father for almost twenty years and never came to know him. Regardless, I honour him for his service to our country in World War Two. Maybe that experience was why my father could not deal with the war that raged in our home. He would see me running around serving my younger siblings, cleaning all the time, wearing rags that were not fit to be used for cleaning, but he said nothing. He played with my older and younger siblings, but seemed to have no room in his heart for my older brother and me. So yes, I hated him. I also grew to hate my older siblings. After they got married and came back to visit, they and their spouses would see me in my rags. They could not help but see what was going on, yet they did nothing to correct the situation. Every time one of the in-laws came to the house and saw me with the broom in my hand, I was embarrassed and ashamed because of what I was wearing. One sister-in-law described the image she had of me as a teenager, standing in the hallway with a broom in my hand. She is kind enough not to mention the rags I was wearing. When in-laws or visitors came to visit, I had to hide in a closet or in the basement until they left. It was appalling that they could be so complacent about what was going on. Why did they not speak up? They saw and knew what was happening. Why didn't they help? I do recall one time when one of my older brothers and his wife took Joseph shopping for clothes. I don't remember all the circumstances, but I do remember that when they came home with Joseph, my parents were absolutely livid. Voices were raised and my parents accused them of interfering in how Joseph was being raised. I don't know if he was allowed to keep the clothes or if they were returned to the store. I believe that from that moment on my brother and his wife were bullied into silence, and they passed that message on to the rest of my siblings. Never again did anyone try to interfere. Consequently, they all became spectators of the abuse unfolding around them. As I shared with you, the children of my siblings were now in the care of my mother, and I think they lived with the fear that if they crossed or disappointed her, she would take out that disappointment on their children, and the cycle of abuse would continue into the next generation. So it seemed the best action was to pretend to be ignorant of what went on in the home and remain silent.

I also learned to hate my younger siblings. I hated them because they were loved, because they all belonged to sports teams, and were permitted to become cubs and scouts. I hated them because their birthdays were celebrated with cakes; they had friends to spend time with and could always get permission to go to their friends' houses. They saw what was happening and often participated in the abuse and name-calling.

As I have stated earlier: to me, my mother was a monster. I believe she hated me, but I will never know why. She was like a chameleon—loving and charming to her husband and her other children one minute, and a monster to me the next. In the twinkling of an eye she could change. I don't think she ever let her husband or her older sons see the true rage that lurked within her. I desperately wanted her love and approval and did everything in my power to get her to love me. I cleaned things for hours—sometimes until my hands were raw—so she would love me. I would try to memorize all my schoolwork so that my marks would please her. I would do my best not to cry, scream, or show any emotion as her blows pummelled my body. I only wanted her to love me, but instead her heart was filled with hate and animosity toward me. And so my heart also became full of hate. Physical, mental, verbal and emotional abuses were all the evil things that happened to me. However, I was also subjected to two other kinds of abuse in our home.

CHAPTER FIVE
Spiritual Abuse

"You are a nasty sinner. You have been marked by the devil and you are going to go straight to hell when you die. God doesn't love you; God can't love you, because you are so wicked!"

From an early age, I was convinced by others that I was a rotten miserable sinner, the worst sinner in the world; that fact was drilled into my head daily. For me to understand what that meant, I was told I had to suffer like Jesus. One of my many punishments was to stand next to a wall without touching it, with my feet together and my arms outstretched so I would know what Jesus felt as He hung on the cross. I was told that Jesus was crucified because I was so bad, and every time I sinned, I was driving the nails further and further into His hands and feet and I was making Him bleed.

I think I was three or four years old the first time I was punished in this way. I wasn't allowed to touch the wall with any part of my body; I had to maintain that position, and it did not take very long before my shoulders and arms ached with weariness. When my arms fell down, a slap or a belt would quickly force them up again. Unfortunately, it did not bring me closer to Jesus; in fact, it made me resent Him. Behind the closed doors of this good Catholic home, physical, emotional, mental, verbal and spiritual abuse took place on a daily basis. I do not know which form of abuse was the most damaging.

As far back as I can remember, prayer and church were integral to our family life. Every morning we said a Catholic litany, and every evening—after the regular beatings—we said the Rosary. Every Sunday we were in church and during Lent, it felt as though we were in church for forty days and forty nights, or perhaps that was just my perception. Religion was a vital part of our routine, but we were certainly not a family who had what I would call a living and active relationship with God. We were a religious family dutifully carrying out the requirements needed to satisfy what we believed was a very angry God. In my mind, if my parents' lives represented God, then He must have been angry and constantly filled with wrath. So I held God fully responsible and blamed Him for what went on inside our home.

We were taught from a young age to fear God and the devil, although as children we were not sure who was more powerful. We believed both of them to be omnipresent and omniscient. When we lived in Sydney, Nova Scotia, there was a church building that housed both Catholic and Protestant congregations. One door led into the Catholic side and the other door into the Protestant side. As Catholics, we were told never to open the door to the Protestant side of the church. Being curious, one day I did just that, and was shocked by two things: first, I was not struck dead; second, Jesus was not on the Cross. I had always been told that only Roman Catholics would go to heaven and everyone else was going to hell. It was every Roman Catholic's task in life to convert those who were not Catholic to Catholicism. However, I was never told the difference between being Catholic or Protestant and any other religious group.

In Sydney, in the Catholic side of the church there was a huge crucifix, which depicted Jesus with blood pouring from His head, hands, feet and side. It was paint, but as a child I believed it was blood, and I did everything I could to avoid looking at the Cross. I was riddled with guilt by the flowing blood and the poor teaching that said every time I sinned, I was wounding Jesus all over again. It made me so aware of how many sins I had committed and how far I had fallen short of God's expectations. I do not know if that was the teaching of the Catholic Church at the time or if the teaching we received at home was just so distorted. All I know is that I begged God to make me a good little boy so I would stop wounding Jesus and that the beatings and the punishment at home would stop. Unfortunately, God did not seem to hear the cry of my heart.

I thought the devil lived in our house—at least that is what we were told, and there were times I certainly believed it. My brother Joseph suffered terribly from abscessed teeth. In our large family, we could not afford to go to the dentist every time one of us had a toothache, and in those days no dental plan existed. So Joseph's teeth would become infected. Sometimes the pain would be so extreme, he would waken in the middle of the night screaming. This would rouse the whole household, but he was never taken to the dentist or the hospital. The infection would cause his cheek to swell. When he woke in the morning with a swollen cheek, he would be told the devil had come and kissed him in the middle of the night. Remember, we shared the same bed, so imagine living with that image in your head night after night. Joseph and I were told we were so bad that the devil would come and take our souls, and that by kissing my brother, he was marking him for hell. So night after night I would barricade our closet door and lie awake with my eyes fixed on it in case the devil emerged. This may seem comical now, but as children, the idea that because we were so bad we were marked for hell by the devil himself tormented us. I fought night after night not to close my eyes so I could remain on guard duty until morning.

Once I became gravely ill, with hives all over my body, but I was not taken to the doctor or the hospital. I was told that I had developed hives because the food I had stolen and eaten was bad. I was so sick that I just wanted to die. I remember waking up from my fever to find Joseph kneeling beside my bed, pleading and bargaining with God that he would be willing to die in my place if God would make me well. That is one of the reasons why my brother was my hero.

Unexpectedly I found a second hero. In 1963, the movie *The Great Escape*, starring Steve McQueen, was a huge box office hit. I was ten years old at the time, and against all odds I was allowed to go and see the movie. This movie was about Allied prisoners of war and how they escaped from a German POW camp in Eastern Poland. Steve McQueen became my hero, as he was the one sent out to scout the lay of the land and then allow himself to be recaptured, so that he could report back. Every time he was captured, he was sent to the cooler, and on his way someone would throw him his baseball glove and ball. The door would close and Steve McQueen would bounce the ball against the wall again and again until the day he was let out and returned to the general population. In my childhood fantasies, I became Steve McQueen. I knew that one day I would escape my prison, and in the meantime I would suffer in silence as my ball bounced against the wall of my prison cell again and again.

As I got older, I remember my anger at God increased. I could not do anything that pleased my mother and I took my anger out on God. I no longer prayed, and when I went to church, I only went through the motions. My brother and I were the family scapegoats, and God was *my* scapegoat, so I would moan and rail against Him for the injustices we were suffering. As I have said, Sunday, the Lord's Day, was my garbage day. I looked on it as God administering the punishment through my mother because I was so evil. To retaliate and to punish Him, I did the two things I had been told never to do as a Catholic: first, I was told never to go to Holy Communion unless I was in what was referred to as a *state of grace*. That meant that I had to confess and repent of all my sins. There was so much anger and bitterness in my soul against my parents and God that I never found myself to be in a state of grace. When I walked down the aisle to receive Communion, I would blaspheme God in my heart. I didn't have any choice in receiving, for if I did not, I would be severely beaten when I got home for shaming the family by remaining in the pew. The second thing we were told was never to let our teeth touch or bite down on the Communion host, because if we did, we were making Jesus bleed. All I wanted to do was to hurt God and make Him feel physical pain the way I was feeling physical pain, so I would bite down on the host with all my might. In hindsight, these were extremely childish things to do, but it was the only way that I could find to lash out at God.

Most beatings that I endured came at the hands of my mother. Although my father did not beat me often, apart from the beating I received from him when accused of stealing my brother's watch, there is another I will never forget. It happened one Sunday morning. My brother and I had been sent off to the early service. It was a typical Sunday morning 8:00 service, and the church was nearly empty. In order for the priest to celebrate communion in the Catholic Church, he needed a server. All my other brothers were permitted to be servers, but Joseph and I were not. On this particular Sunday, the priest called one of us to come forward to serve. Joseph whispered to me that we would be beaten if we dared go forward. Feeling brave, I thought, *what harm would it do?* The priest needed a server, and I had watched my siblings do it often enough, so for me it was absolutely no problem. When my parents found out, my father beat me severely. I can't remember if he used his belt or his hand, but I do know it hurt, and to this day I still do not know what I did wrong. That caused me to harden my heart even more towards my parents and towards God whom I had served at the altar.

Many other incidents of spiritual abuse took place in our home; however, what I have shared gives you some idea of the distorted and dysfunctional religious environment in which I was raised. As much as I hated God, I also feared Him. As I got older, I knew that God had the power to annihilate me at any moment, but I had no way of releasing my anger against Him. I had no one to talk to—no one who might explain the great frustration and rage that was erupting in my heart. Who could understand the depth of my anger? Who could deliver me from this torment? Young as I was, I knew I needed someone to stand between me and God to present my case. But that was not to happen. It seemed as if God was never going to *deliver me from evil.*

CHAPTER SIX
Sexual Abuse

"Someone please come home . . . God, please hide me; please make him go away."

I hear his steps coming closer.

"I'll hold my breath . . . please don't let him hear me."

Suddenly, he grabs one of my feet and pulls me out from underneath the bed.

"Oh, there you are! Come with me—I have a doughnut for you. Don't you want your doughnut? I bought it especially for you. Come on, let's go down to the bathroom and eat our doughnuts together."

In earlier chapters, I have described the physical, emotional, mental, verbal and spiritual abuse that I endured for close to twenty years. I was also the victim of a sexual predator who had open access to our home in Sydney, Nova Scotia. I used to think that if I hid under the bed he would not find me, but that did not deter him. To this day, I can hear him opening bedroom and closet doors looking for me.

I did not realize that he was a predator. Almost thirty years later over a dinner in Vancouver, I shared very nervously with one of my older siblings what this man did to me. His immediate response was, "Oh, he was and is a sexual predator and always will be." I was so incredibly naïve. As a child, I had no idea what the expression *sexual predator* meant. Merriam-Webster defines a sexual predator as "a person who has committed a sexually violent offence and especially one who is likely to commit more sexual offences."[6] This sexual predator had free access to us children, and I know for a fact that I wasn't his only victim. But others will have to tell their own stories; they are not for me to tell.

As I work my way through this book, I have consulted with those whose wisdom I deeply value. I have been hesitant to share the details of my abuse. However, my counselling mentors have suggested that I include details of all the abuse, including the sexual abuse, as this may help those who have suffered in similar ways. In my case, the predator forced me to perform fellatio on him. Imagine what that does to a child! For many years I lived with a choking sensation and a constant feeling that I was unclean. I still believe that I took up the habit of smoking to try to rid myself of the taste and the sense of uncleanliness. When I finally faced the truth about the sexual abuse, I was able to quit smoking. That was over twenty years ago. I endured this sexual abuse weekly and it started when I was about five. It continued until I was ten or eleven and then he moved away and I was safe.

6 http://www.merriam-webster.com/dictionary/sexualpredator

Fifty years later, some details remain murky. Why are some details so clear and others rather vague? There are two major reasons: first, a person who has been sexually abused does not want to remember the unpleasant details. The victim desperately wants the abuse to stop. Within them a silent scream tears their soul apart. Fifty years later, I feel really ill if I think about it. Secondly, victims of sexual abuse, especially those who suffer this indignity on a continuous basis, tend to break off from themselves. They know that something horrible is being done to their body, but emotionally and mentally they are no longer present. They may be outside the room or watching from the ceiling, but they are no longer part of the event. As a result of this splitting off or going away, victims of sexual abuse find it extremely difficult to form intimate relationships with those who genuinely love them. They avoid direct eye contact and remain on guard for years. They do so because they think others can see inside their souls and know that they have been damaged.

Predators may lure their victim with doughnuts or other treats, but these are merely a bribe; they are not at all interested in rewarding their victims. Nor are they concerned about the victim's feelings. The abuse is all about them, satisfying their lust and ensuring their pleasure. Sexual interference with a child by an adult is nothing but exploitation. This exploitation causes tremendous suffering and pain for years to come. Sexual interference is nothing but an indulgence in self-absorption. As someone who has suffered abuse, I confess that I have very little tolerance for adults who exploit children or others to satisfy their lusts.

The predator was well aware of our family's dysfunction. It was very difficult for me; after all, to whom could I turn? For years and years I felt guilty that I was not able to stop the abuse that happened to me or my other siblings. I could not go to my parents or to any other person in the house. I had no other adult in my life, and if I dared suggest to any outsider that something dark and evil was taking place in our home, I knew for certain that I would not be believed. Consequently, the abuse was our little secret and he did not have to tell me not to share this information with anyone. He knew I could not. I was completely in his power and under his control.

Although at times I could mentally and emotionally disappear while the abuse was taking place, waves of helplessness and fear overcame me every time he forced me into the bathroom with him. It was the only door in the house with a lock and, being a very big man, he could stand with his foot against the door as extra protection, so that no one could possibly enter. The sorrow that remained in my soul for years was the awful realization that while I was being abused, I was filled with shame. The longer the abuse went on, the more I believed that it must be my fault. I believed that I must have done something evil to merit or to attract this kind of attention.

Over the years on my journey to wholeness, I have read extensively and have researched the results of childhood sexual abuse. I am not a qualified therapist or counsellor, but I am one of many who were abused and sexually molested as children. The following random thoughts are from my readings and journals as I worked to find my personal freedom and helped others to find the same.

Experience has told me that when one opens the door to the deepest depths of one's soul, you find that recovering from childhood sexual abuse is a lifelong project. As you work your way through the stifling accumulation of hurt, pain, sorrow, disappointment and regret that have become part of you, often those feelings play themselves out in real time. Furthermore, these memories are impossible to share except with those in whom you have developed a deep trust. I know that when I finally began to share with my therapists and my spouse I would at times weep uncontrollably. I wasn't weeping for myself; I was weeping for my family and for the awful secrets they have been forced to carry from one generation to another.

We must understand that these kinds of events are not to be casually shared with just anyone. My therapists and my spouse have watched me struggle with recurring nightmares and flashbacks, especially when I spend time in the basement of my soul. I use the term *basement* to describe the deep place in my memory that I must re-enter if I hope to become whole. Cognitively I recognize that I am taking this journey as an adult, but from time to time I still feel like a frightened little boy, trapped in that bathroom. However, I am willing to risk going to the basement, because I yearn to be whole and to help others on their journey to wholeness. I do not want to live my life or see others live their lives as confused and frightened children, never reaching their full potential as human beings. I am so grateful to my generous and empathetic wife that she did not dismiss or make light of the suffering I endured. When I wept, while writing this book, she wept with me, which was the greatest gift I could have received from another person.

Over the years of my reading and study, which I recorded in my journals, I unfortunately did not list all the books, tapes, and other resources I used. However, the Appendix does list some of these resources that others may find helpful. My personal studies through the years as I pursued wholeness revealed four basic facts, which I will describe very, very briefly:

First, we need to be aware that every child knows that sexual touching with an adult is a secret, a shameful secret. So not only are they shamed, they also carry a tremendous amount of guilt, because something inside them tells them the behaviour is wrong. In time, as they mature and face up to what has been done to them, they know that their abuser neither valued nor respected them, but merely used them for their own gratification. Any affection shown was false.

This leads to the second fact: sexual abuse is one of the greatest betrayals that can take place between an adult and a child. Children instinctively seek safe places to be or safe people to be with. When you find out that a safe person turns out to be a predator, the betrayal cuts very deep.

Third, according to experts, children below the age of approximately eleven (I personally think it should be much older) should never be sexually awakened. They are not developmentally ready for any kind of emotional, physical, or sexual relationship. They should be carefree and encouraged by adults to know what it means to be a little boy or a little girl. Sexual interference causes abused children to perceive themselves as a sexual object of little value to anyone, except as an object of pleasure.

Fourth, a child trapped in a sexual relationship with an adult is completely powerless. The adult holds all the power, and everything in that relationship is built around the needs of the adult. As the child grows up and realizes what has happened, they are overwhelmed with guilt feelings that they should have been able to stop the abuse. They see themselves as weak and useless, and are filled with shame. They think others see them that way too, and as I said before, they find it extremely difficult to maintain eye contact with others. This further isolates them, making them more vulnerable to continued abuse, and to alienation from others as an adult.

Sexual abuse occurs daily in our society. Statistics indicate that one out of every four women and one out of every six men has been sexually abused.[7] I would be bold enough to say that male sexual abuse is for the most part unreported. Having been a victim myself, and after years of counselling and listening to males who have also been victims, there is a devastating sense of shame in anyone who has been sexually abused. Males tend to think that they should have had the strength or ability to stop the predator, even when they were children or teenagers. Since they could not, there is a deep sense of disgrace and humiliation. You cannot imagine telling anyone what has been done to you, especially when it happened in a home or a setting where you felt there was no safe person to turn to. It is my personal opinion that a male trying to face the reality of sexual abuse while weighed down by inordinate grief feels the shame more deeply. The grief encompasses the loss of innocence, the powerlessness, and the worthlessness that constantly burdens the soul. What the predators never realize is the damage they do. They rob people of intimacy; some of their victims commit suicide, some become institutionalized, and still others swim in oceans of pain and torment, day in and day out, because they feel unclean and guilty.

In my case, the sad reality is that when I was being sexually abused, it was the only time I was ever touched. Was this really the only way in which I was worthy of being touched? So from a very young age I knew about hunger, cold, danger and desperation. Those were the burdens I carried from my childhood into my adulthood. Those memories were the demons that imprisoned me in chains of fear, guilt, and shame one decade after another. When I finally left home, I hated my father, my mother, my siblings, and the sexual predator that had damaged

7 http:1in6.org/family-and-friends/myths
www.jimhopper.com

my body, my soul, and my spirit. I hated them all, but the sexual predator gave me yet another reason to hate God.

More than anyone else, I blamed God for placing me in this family and permitting this evil to take place. I loathed my life and I loathed God. I hated God with a passion that could not be expressed in words. If I could have had my hands around His throat, I would have throttled Him. I would have whipped and beaten Him. I would have volunteered to join those at the crucifixion. I would have driven the nails into His hands and feet and have thrust the spear into His side. I would have pulled out His beard and I would have forced the crown of thorns upon His head with all my strength. Perhaps then, my anger would have abated.

CHAPTER SEVEN
Leaving Home

"You should go out to work and pay rent. We have worked hard to provide your food, clothing, and a roof over your head, and now you should contribute and pay us back for supporting you all these years. You should be grateful for all we have given you."

Given me? What did I receive? As a result of living in that mess for almost twenty years, I had developed a heart of stone the size of a huge boulder. My stony heart was abrasive and seemed to fill my entire chest. I had no self-esteem, no sense of identity, no sense of hope or a future, and I constantly felt rejected. I was filled with sorrow. I felt like garbage. Dressed in my rags, I looked like garbage. Starving, I ate garbage. Sunday after Sunday, I lived in garbage. I was an angry man. Although I did not realize it, I had been raised to be an angry man, and now I was let loose on the world. After almost twenty years of physical, mental, verbal, emotional, spiritual and sexual abuse, it was time for me to escape. But the problem was, I had no idea how to escape; I wasn't equipped. Yes, I knew I was supposed to leave, but I was too insecure and filled with paralyzing fear, despite all those years of telling myself I was going to leave at the first opportunity I had. I was confused; I was frustrated; I lived with hopelessness, with pain, with regrets; I was so very sad, and although constantly surrounded by people I was extremely lonely. My upbringing did not equip me for the world.

What did I learn in that house of horrors? I suppose, more than anything else, I learned responsibility. It had been drummed into me that I was not allowed to rest or have fun. I always had to appear busy, and if I was not busy, I was made busy. Fun was for the others, and if I did have fun, I had to be very careful that I would not be caught. The clear expectation was that now I was to set off into the world and earn my living, pretending the first twenty years of my life had been times of positive maturing and of joy and peace. I was never to speak about what went on behind the doors of our house, and whenever I came home, God forbid that I would ever mention the past. My worldview was badly distorted. I thought the behaviour that went on in my house was the norm. It was not until years later I realized that it was the exception and not the rule. Finally away from home, I watched other parents interact with their children, and could see and sense the genuine love and caring between them. I certainly envied their relationships.

I finished high school in 1972 and I had no idea what I wanted to do with my life. I had never thought that far ahead. All I had wanted to do was get through the day. In my environment, I only had to plan minute by minute, hour by hour, or day by day. Now the school year was over and I was expected to go off and earn a living. When I left school I had no friends as I was not permitted to form friendships. I didn't belong to groups or to clubs. I was all alone. There would be no point in me going back to a school reunion as I am positive that no-one would recognize me or even remember my name. After school, there was definitely no thought of university, even though for others in the family, that was their next step. But it was the workforce for me. I knew nothing about finding a job, renting an apartment, buying clothes and food, getting a driver's licence and being a responsible adult. The world terrified me. I knew my home was unsafe but I also believed the world was unsafe. In 1963 the world was shocked by the assassination of John F. Kennedy. I recall to this day being so shocked I dared at recess to sit down on the back steps of the school. I remember weeping for him. I thought if people could kill the president of the United States, they could easily kill me, and so the world was not safe; thus I concluded that I'd better stick close to home.

I remember the first time I went downtown to apply for a job. I had fifty cents in my pocket—bus fare there and bus fare home. When I finished my interview I walked outside the building in downtown Ottawa and a street person asked me for twenty-five cents to buy a cup of coffee. (Yes, that was possible in those days.) I gave him my twenty-five cents and walked a block before I suddenly realized that I had no way to get home. I knew Cynthia worked downtown and I knew her work address, so I walked thirty blocks to her office and she gave me the money to get home. I was that naïve!

With no firm plan in mind, I eventually took a job with the government in the mailroom at the National Research Council (NRC), which was not very far from my house. After I took the job I realized that I had deliberately chosen a place close to my house as I was terrified to be out in the world. I didn't know how to act; I didn't know how to make friends; I didn't know how to open a bank account; I didn't know what to do with money, since I had never had any before. In fact, the only thing I knew was how to work. But it didn't take me long to become completely bored with delivering mail from building to building. Outside the NRC was a very large glass sphere, and my father would tell people it was my job to polish, dust, and shine it on a daily basis. Some would say he was teasing, but I found his comments demeaning.

The time came when I finally knew that I desperately needed to get away from home, but I didn't know what to do, until the day I saw a recruiting sign for the Canadian Armed Forces. When I went in to apply, all they were looking for at that time was infantrymen and navy personnel. I had no desire for either, but I do remember crying out to God to get me into the military and get me away from home. A week later, my prayer was answered when they called me back and told me that they were now recruiting for administrative personnel. That is what I had studied in high school; I was more than qualified, and they readily accepted me. Before I knew it, I was off to basic training in Cornwallis, Nova Scotia, then to Borden, Ontario for trades training, and then to Lahr, West Germany as my first official posting. As embarrassing as it sounds, the day I left home for Cornwallis was the very last day I wet the bed. My bedwetting began when I was child and was sent to bed at 5:30 p.m., and under no circumstances was I permitted to get out of that bed until the next morning. It is amazing what fear does to the human body, even after you start growing from a child to a teenager and finally to an adult!

Years later, my sister Annie shared with me that she was terrified when I joined the military. She told me that when she heard this news she lived in absolute terror, convinced that when I had access to a gun, I would come home and kill the entire family. My loving sister was sure that my anger could easily have distorted me into becoming a killer. When you are angry, you may think that no one else knows what you are feeling. When I observe someone who is angry, there are many red flags—body language, tone of voice, choice of words, facial expressions and the colour of their face convey the degree of their anger. When my sister shared her fears about me killing our family, I realized my anger was very obvious. I now realize that I must have seemed like a stick of dynamite ready to explode.

However, it never occurred to me to do such an evil thing. To this day I remain convinced that the military saved my sanity and my life. I was finally free from the chains that had bound me. The military gave me a sense of stability, companionship, and purpose. Now I was as far away from home as possible. You would think that I would be deliriously happy, but I wasn't. I carried my duffle bags of unhappiness with me. When I first arrived in Germany, I was overwhelmingly lonely—believe it or not—for the only family I had ever known. Night after night I cried myself to sleep with the ache of loneliness in my soul. I could not wait to get away, but when I was finally far enough away to feel safe, I pined for home. Hard to imagine, but that was the sad reality. I thought that my family might miss me and that since I was away and had made a responsible career choice they would love me, but unfortunately that was not the case.

I was following, although not consciously, in my father's footsteps. Maybe I joined the military so I would have something in common with my father, the stranger. I thought surely I would have the approval, acceptance, and love of my parents, but that was a great illusion. In the first year I was stationed overseas, I returned home for Christmas, laden down with presents for the whole family. I know now that I was trying to win their love and affection and show everyone what a success I was. Although I was not beaten, punished, or sent to my room with no supper,

I was shunned, and the same sarcastic remarks followed me day in and day out. Nothing had changed; the reactions were exactly the same. I remember to this day thinking, *I just want you to love me; please, can't you just love me?*

I went back to Germany with the attitude that I would show them. I would be the best soldier the military had ever produced. During the next twenty-four months, I completed every project the military assigned me. In fact, I did them exceptionally well—so much so that after twenty-four months on the main base, I was posted internally to 444 Tactical Helicopter Squadron, and as a result of my work on the base, I received an accelerated promotion to corporal, which normally took forty-eight months. I thought, *surely now my family will be proud of me*, but my status and rank in the military were never mentioned.

My anger with God did not go away when I left home. Even though I had pleaded with Him to get me into the military, the first thing I gave up when I was far from home was church, even on special occasions. For a Catholic who had spent a lifetime in the church, the guilt was overwhelming, but I refused to succumb to it. On the first Good Friday I was away from home, I went into a restaurant and deliberately ordered a steak. In those days, Catholics did not eat meat on Friday, and absolutely *never* on Good Friday. The restaurant refused to give me a steak as they were observing Good Friday. My pettiness should give you an idea of the hostility I carried. This incident told me that I needed to do something to get rid of the bitterness in my soul against God.

I decided to attempt to get my life right with God and attended church for about three weeks. The Catholic padre was to lead a trip to Lourdes, France, the place where the Virgin Mary appeared to three young children in 1858. He invited me along, saying he was taking only the best male Catholics from the base.

I think because I was new to the base and single, he decided that I should go. However, I was completely overwhelmed by the poverty of those who came looking for a miracle of healing, in contrast to the richness of the priest's vestments and the chalices used for celebrating the Sacrament. On the way home, most of the "best" Catholics on the trip were drunk and disorderly. They shouted obscenities at each other across the aisles and were rude and obnoxious. If these were the best Catholics, I wanted nothing to do with them. I had enough hypocrisy to last me a lifetime when I was growing up; I didn't need it in my new life. After that misadventure, I was determined it would be the last time I would darken the doors of a church.

I remember another incident that took place in Germany. I wanted to talk to the chaplain as I was still struggling with my baggage of sorrow, regret, frustration and anger that I had carried from home. The rules were quite explicit at that time: if you were Catholic, you spoke to the Catholic padre; if you were Protestant, you spoke to the Protestant padre. When I went to the church office, the Protestant padre would not see me and told me to wait for the Catholic padre. The Catholic padre did not show up and so, desperate to find out about God, I left the office, and on the way past the Protestant chapel I stole a Bible. I brought it back to the barracks and tried to read it and make sense of it, but it was the King James Version of the Bible in old English. I found this very confusing. I kept it as a good luck charm, even though the contents did not make sense to me. I put it under my pillow, hoping that by osmosis its message would creep into my head and heart. Although I did not realize it at the time, this was my first genuine effort to try to find a real relationship with God.

I enjoyed my three years in Germany, but to my regret, when my tour was up, I was posted back to Ottawa. As there were no barracks available in the Ottawa area, I had to move back home. My mother expected me to live at home and pay rent. It was the last place I wanted to be, but given the circumstances, I felt I had no choice. About six months after my posting back to Ottawa I desperately needed to escape, so I did a very foolish thing: I decided to get married.

I had met a young girl in Germany—Doreen, daughter of a warrant officer who was now stationed in Ottawa. I believed I was in love with her. When I told my mother my exciting news, the first thing she said was, "Don't be so foolish!" I felt rebuked and hurt that even at the age of twenty-four I had no control over my life. So I took control. Did I love Doreen? To this day, I do not know, because I had no idea what love was. All I knew was that once again my mother was interfering in my life, and so I was determined to marry Doreen regardless. All around me I observed my workmates and my siblings getting married, and I thought I should also get married. If nothing else, it would get me out of that house. Doreen was eighteen years old and as immature as I was. Looking back and gauging our maturity, Doreen was in some ways only twelve years old, and I was maybe fifteen years old. She looked like a little china doll and I wanted to protect her. I knew when I walked down the aisle that marrying her was probably not the wisest way to get out of the house, but at the time it seemed to be the only way. Nine months after we were married, the military posted me to Alert in the Northwest Territories. It is the most northerly isolated posting that the military has, and I was to be stationed there for six months with 250 other men.

After we were married, we made friends with a family in our apartment building, Bill, his wife Sandra and their son William. Bill was my first really close friend and I trusted him completely. I asked him to keep an eye on Doreen so that she would be all right while I was away. Doreen had been a military child and was used to her father and her brother going off on isolated postings. It was the way of life in the military.

While I was in Alert, the one thing that kept me going was receiving mail. Those were the days before personal computers, cell phones, Skype, Twitter, and other forms of social media. The mail came weekly with a new batch of personnel as the base was on a constant rotation. Mail was what one lived for. About three months into my posting, I stopped receiving mail. I was not overly concerned at first, but after two or three weeks, I knew something was wrong. The only other means of communication was by short-wave radio from Alert to Ottawa. This could not be private as two operators would be listening in at all times. When I called Doreen she was not very responsive, but we could not say much on the radio. When I came home in August, she told me that things were fine, that she had gone through a difficult time and was not able to write, so I let it go. I carried on and spent countless hours with my best friend playing baseball and golf. I had been home for two months when the military promoted me to master corporal and sent me on a six-week course to Borden, Ontario.

One night during a phone call to Doreen from Borden, she tearfully confessed to me that she had been carrying on a relationship with someone else while I was stationed in Alert. That was why my mail had suddenly stopped. She said, "You had competition while you were away, but it is over." It had never crossed my mind that something like that would ever happen. I asked her who it was. She told me it had been with my best friend Bill, but it was over. When I returned to Ottawa, I discovered that the relationship was far from over. Many evenings, when Doreen was supposedly out with girlfriends, she was with Bill. When I confronted her, I could see that she was totally committed to him. His marriage had broken up; his wife and child had moved out and he was alone. I knew he would not be alone for long, and so I asked Doreen to choose between us. I was not surprised when she chose Bill—after all, wasn't I the unlovable one? At least that is what I had been taught, and here was the proof. I could not even hold onto my marriage.

That night, I called my older brother, the one who rescued me from under the trap door of our house in Sydney, Nova Scotia. I asked him if I could come and stay the night. He fixed me up a bed and I remember crying as I had never cried before. I felt as though my heart was literally breaking. Even after all I had been through, I had never felt so betrayed. Over the course of the next several weeks, I begged and pleaded with Doreen to reconsider, but she was totally convinced that Bill was the man she had been waiting for all her life. Shortly after this she informed me she was pregnant. In spite of this, I offered again to reconcile and said that we could raise the child as our own, but she desperately wanted a divorce. The door was permanently closed and my heart was shattered.

So here I was, twenty-six years old, and my life was a complete and total disaster. Doreen and Bill's betrayal confirmed that I was unlovable. My parents didn't love me, my wife of less than two short years didn't love me, my best friend betrayed me, and I was all alone. If I had ever hoped to win my parents' love, that dream was now shattered. In this good Catholic family, I was now the divorced one. How had I dared to do that and shame the family? Despite the circumstances, I had failed yet again! I was forsaken, betrayed, and thrown to the dogs. What was I to do now?

I thought my only option was to find a way to kill myself. The pain was too much, and all I wanted to do was lie down and die and finally be at rest. In this state of despair, I thought that

God was after me because I had committed so many sins, and that He had offered a reward for my capture, dead or alive. I was still technically a Catholic and had been taught that if I took my life it would be an unforgivable sin; I would be buried in unconsecrated ground, and forced to wander the earth for eternity. I thought if I could find a way to stage an accident so that no one would know that it was suicide, somehow I could also fool God into believing it was an accident. If I drove my car into a barrier on the highway, no one would know it was deliberate—and, more importantly, neither would God.

I fell into a deep depression and did not know what to do. If I sought the help of military chaplains or military psychiatrists, I could kiss goodbye whatever career I had in the military. I did not know how severe my depression was; all I knew was that I wanted to die, but I did not dare tell others the depths of my despair. Every day I dragged myself to work, and at night I walked the streets of the city until I was exhausted. I could not believe that my life had turned out this way. What could I do? I felt absolutely hopeless.

However, my story would not end on a note of despair. As it turns out, this would be one of many more chapters in the story of my life.

Part II

DAMASCUS ROAD

May 29, 1979 – March 1, 1994

“For you created my inmost being;
You knit me together in my mother’s womb.
I praise you because I am fearfully
And wonderfully made;
Your works are wonderful
I know that full well.
My frame was not hidden from you
When I was made in the secret place,
When I was woven together in
The depths of the earth.
Your eyes saw my unformed body;
All the days ordained for me were
Written in your book
Before one of them came to be.
How precious to me are your
Thoughts, God
How vast is the sum of them.”
(Psalm 139:13 –17)

CHAPTER EIGHT
A New Life

"Then Jesus told them this parable. Suppose one of you has a hundred sheep and loses one of them. Doesn't he leave the ninety-nine in the open country and go after the lost sheep until he finds it? And when he finds it, he joyfully puts it on his shoulders and goes home. Then he calls his friends and neighbors together and says; Rejoice with me; I have found my lost sheep. I tell you that in the same way there will be more rejoicing in heaven over one sinner who repents than over ninety-nine righteous persons who do not need to repent." (Luke 15:3-7)

Although I did not make any serious attempts to take my own life, I desperately wanted to die and constantly thought about it. In many ways I was a walking dead man; I had absolutely nothing to live for. My family had rejected me from birth, the woman I thought I loved rejected me, and my best friend betrayed me. So I started looking for some meaning in my life. I knew I had to find God, even though I thought that He might destroy me. My abusive background taught me that God was not good, but for some reason, despite my history, I was still willing to risk an encounter. I somehow still believed that the God who supposedly ran the universe was the only one who could give me the answers I was seeking.

So, where could I, a young Catholic man, go looking for God? To start, I went back to the church I had discarded when I went to Germany, but I did not go to services. I drove around the city at night visiting as many Catholic churches as I could find. In those days, the churches were not locked. I went in to these churches, knelt down, and poured my heart out to an unknown God. I thought if ever I was going to find God, it would be in a Roman Catholic church, for I had been taught that is where God lived exclusively. I lost count of the number of churches I wandered in and out of, but I could not rest until I had confronted God. I was convinced God was punishing me because I was such a bad person and that He would not be satisfied until I was utterly destroyed. In many ways, I wanted to take God into a courtroom and put Him on trial. I wanted God in the witness stand, and I wanted Him to tell me why my life was such a mess. I don't know if I would have listened to Him if He wanted to respond to me. I had already made up my mind that I would find Him guilty! But He couldn't be found, at least not in the places where I was looking.

While I was serving in Alert, Northwest Territories, I found a good friend in Jacques, the station cook. We were the same age, and to pass our time in an isolated posting, we would run around the gymnasium for hours. We became close, and one day he called from Vancouver. He was in the Navy and called with exciting news. While he was in Alert, his wife Suzanne had found Jesus, and now Jacques had also found Him.

"I didn't know Jesus had been lost, so how could He be found?" I asked sarcastically. But Jacques would not be put off. When he asked me how I was, I told him what a disaster my life had become. I told him I felt that I had fallen into a pit from which I would never escape. He in turn told me about Jesus and explained how much I needed to find God in my life and have a personal relationship with Him. I felt like screaming at Jacques and hanging up on him, because as a good Catholic, I thought I knew all there was to know about God. Although I was looking for Him, my purpose was to put Him on trial. I wanted the opportunity to literally shake Him and tell Him how much I despised Him. I was not consciously looking for a personal relationship with Him and I doubted if He was interested in a personal relationship with me. How dare Jacques tell me that I needed to find Jesus! It was all I could do not to slam the phone down in anger.

Little did I know that Jacques' call marked the day my life began to change. Did I find God and put Him on trial? Did I shake Him until His teeth rattled? No, I did not find Him! Instead, He found me! He did not put me on trial, nor did He shake me until my teeth rattled. He did something so unexpected that thirty-seven years later I remember it as if it happened yesterday. Jacques was so concerned about me that he called a friend of his in Ottawa, who in turn called me that same day. Jacques' friend Calvin told me that Jacques had called; then Calvin invited me out for supper that evening.

What do I have to lose? I thought. Most evenings I wandered the streets of Ottawa, going in and out of churches, looking for my elusive unknown God. After work that day, I was picked up by Calvin and driven to a community centre where there was an Athletics in Action[8] banquet. It was one of the strang-

8 Athleticsinaction.com

est events I had ever attended. Everyone seemed overly friendly, but more than anything else I noticed the way they sang the national anthem. I was used to being on a parade square with thousands of others, where, along with a military band, we sang "O Canada." But these people sang "O Canada" as if they loved Canada. It sounded more like a hymn rather than the national anthem. It was a strange and wonderful experience, which I enjoyed immensely. Calvin talked to me all evening about Jesus and the need to have a personal relationship with God. But there was no way that I could understand this concept of having a personal relationship with God. In my upbringing, God was a mysterious being who lived in heaven and was keeping a record of everything I did wrong. He was like a policeman or like my mother, who always seemed to know when I did or even thought something wrong.

Calvin invited me to church the next evening. I thought it was strange having a church service in the middle of the week, but I agreed. I assumed that because I had shared a bit about my church background that we would be going to a special service at a Catholic church—however, that was not the case.

The next evening he picked me up, and we drove to a church in downtown Ottawa. I discovered later on that it was a Pentecostal church. At the time, I had no idea what a Pentecostal church was. I only knew it was a Protestant church and that if I was discovered there by God I would be put on a speeding train going straight to hell. When I walked into the church it was packed, and all the people were singing with their hands in the air. As I had no car and no way to leave, I didn't have any choice but to stay. I decided to sit near the front of the church so that all those nuts with their hands in the air would be behind me. There were no places to kneel, so I sat and prayed to God that if He would forgive me for coming into this church, and if He could get me out, I would never darken the door of a Protestant church again. At that moment, as a Catholic, I believed I was committing an unpardonable sin.

After what seemed like forever, the music stopped, and a football player I had never heard of stood up and began to talk about Jesus. He talked as if Jesus was his very best friend and he knew Him intimately. As he spoke, the whole world disappeared for me. I felt as if I were the only person in the church and that the speaker was addressing me directly. For a time, I forgot all my problems and focused on what the speaker was saying about the possibility of being in a personal relationship with God. But it was more than that. I don't know when it happened, but at some point I suddenly recognized an awesome presence in the building, and it felt holy.

When this football player was finished, he asked us to close our eyes and said that if we wanted to invite Jesus into our lives, all we had to do was raise our hands and He would come in. I sat in the pew and prayed, *God, I have tried just about everything else; why not try this, Jesus? At this point in my life, I have nothing to lose.* I put my hand up in the air and the power of God fell on me. In a split second, my life changed.

The best way for me to describe it is like this: the next time you step into a hot shower and the water cascades down over you, stop for a moment and experience that sensation. That is exactly what it felt like to me. Over and over and over again I was immersed and bathed not only in the power of God, but in the love of God. It was as if the heavens had opened and rain started to fall upon me. The only way to describe the rain is to describe it as the overwhelming love of God. I felt totally flooded with the real and alive presence of God. From the top of my head to the bottom of my feet I was filled with love. In that moment, I knew I was loveable. Not useless, not evil, not four-eyes, and not the family runt and failure. No, I was a loveable child of God. The God of all creation had found me. I did not find Him; He found me. I have no rational or scientific explanation for what happened to me. All I know is that one moment I was completely lost and the next I was found. I was blind, but now I could see. Tears started streaming down my face; I could not stop weeping, and I did not care who saw me. For the very first time in my life, I no longer felt lonely—I felt loved, I felt safe, and felt like I was wrapped in a blanket of peace. Trying to explain this event thirty-seven years later is as difficult now as it was when it happened.

I do not know why I was so blessed. I do not know why God took mercy upon me and reached down and touched me. The closest parallel to this experience that I can find in Scripture was a man named Saul and his Damascus Road experience. Saul was a persecutor of Christ and His followers. He wanted to stamp out the Church and the name of Jesus Christ. He was on the road from Jerusalem on his way to Damascus to hunt down Christians. He had been given a commission by the religious authorities in Jerusalem to find as many Christians as he could, throw them in jail, and have them killed. He had been extremely successful in his missions and had the reputation as the greatest enemy of the Church. As he rode along, he was thrown off his horse. A light from heaven flashed all around him and he heard a voice saying, "Saul, Saul, why do you persecute me?"

"Who are you, Lord?" Saul asked.

"I am Jesus whom you are persecuting."[9]

And so Saul was struck blind until a man in the Church in Damascus came and laid hands on him and baptized him in the name of Jesus Christ. Saul's life was transformed and, as a result, his name was changed. He became Paul, the Apostle, and

9 Acts 9:5-6

God entrusted him with writing most of the New Testament. Although I was not a persecutor of the Church, I certainly was a persecutor of God. One moment I despised Him; I had mocked Him and, on a regular basis, had blasphemed His name. It was so bad that one day Joseph said to me, "Why do you curse and swear and constantly take the Lord's name in vain?" I knew I did those things because I was angry and bitter at God, and to curse and blaspheme Him was the only way that I knew to effectively strike out at Him. One moment I was a blasphemer, and the next I was filled with love for Him. Only God could do that!

After my experience, which I know now was the outpouring of the Holy Spirit, the speaker asked those who had accepted Jesus to come forward; someone would pray with us to be sure that Christ was now part of our lives. (See the Appendix for the actual prayer I prayed that night.) I went forward, and it turned out that the man who prayed with me was Gerry Organ, the former place-kicker for the Ottawa Rough Riders. As he prayed with me, he told me that God had a wonderful plan for my life. I could not imagine how this could be possible. After all, I had been taught that I was unlovable, and that God was a God of wrath and anger, not a God of love. But it was a God of love that I had just experienced that night. I could walk out of that church knowing for the first time in my life that God was real and that God was love.

That night I shared with those who brought me to church that all I wanted to do was spend the rest of my life telling people about Jesus. You may think that this is ludicrous and that I was just overwhelmed by emotion. Yes, I was very emotional that night. However, since that night the thought of sharing the Good News with others has burned in my heart and mind. At twenty-six years old, I *finally found the purpose* for which I had been born. Since then, that is all I have wanted to do. Calvin and the others did not understand, any more than I did, what had happened to me. They did not know enough about me to understand my whole life had just been turned completely upside down. In that service, God performed a miracle, and my life was transformed. That night, as far as I could recall, was the first time I went to bed without fear and woke up the next morning with a craving for life. I had finally found the purpose for my existence, and sharing Jesus and the Scriptures with others has remained my passion ever since. Yes, the fire that started in my heart that night still burns within me today.

When I went into my office the next day, a co-worker took one look and me and asked, "What happened to you?" I had spent months and months dragging myself to work, and it was probably obvious to others that I was severely depressed. It must also have been obvious to them on this day that something very different had happened to me. I said the first thing that came to my mind: "Last night, I found out that Jesus Christ is alive." She looked at me as if I had three heads. Her reaction amazed me as I was convinced the whole world apart from me knew about Jesus. I thought I was the only one who lived in darkness. But that day I discovered that much of the world, and many of those who thought they were living, were actually as dead as I had been before May 29, 1979.

After my conversion my family thought that I had gone off the deep end. In my enthusiasm, I spent a lot of my time just talking about Jesus and telling them that they each needed to have a relationship with Him. I was now courageous enough to start looking for my own place to live. I no longer felt frightened by the world. However, my brother Joseph invited me to live with him, his wife, and their new son. Before I moved in, he said to me, "The only rule is you cannot talk to us about this Jesus stuff." I promised I would not. The night I moved in, Joseph came downstairs to see how I had set up my living quarters. He noticed a book by Billy Graham entitled *How to be Born Again* on my bookshelf. He took it to read, and that very night He was converted to Christ and his life was transformed. (I have told you this story now, and you will understand why in the last chapter of this book.)

The day after my conversion, I went to the local Christian bookstore and purchased a copy of the King James Version of the Bible. Now I had no problem understanding it. It was as if I had been reading it all my life. To my family, friends, and co-workers, I must have appeared for a time to be holier than thou. They could not understand the change in my life any more than I could. But it did not matter to me; what mattered was I was alive and knew beyond a shadow of doubt that God loved me. He had a wonderful plan for my life, but I did not have a clue at that time how much more suffering I would have to endure to be shaped into the man that God wanted me to become. The Apostle Paul had also been warned by God how much he would suffer for the sake of the Gospel. He was told by Ananias, the man from Damascus who had baptized him, of the commission to which God had called him: "This man is my chosen instrument to proclaim my name to the Gentiles and their kings and to the people of Israel. I will show him how much he must suffer for my name."[10]

On the night that God invaded my life I was not thinking about suffering at all. All I knew was that He heard the cry of my heart and climbed down into the slimy pit where I had been living, and He picked me up like a loving father and carried me out of that pit. He set my feet on a rock, and though from time to time I have slipped off the rock and slithered back into the pit,

10 Acts 9:15–16

He has never left me, forgotten me, or forsaken me.[11] However, if I had known what the future held for me, I would have just stayed in that church in downtown Ottawa for the rest of my life and basked in the glory that I had experienced that night. I did not know that the future would bring me so much more suffering. I thought I had experienced more than my fair share in my life thus far. But there was so much more yet to come.

---

11 Psalm 40: 1-2

CHAPTER NINE
Spiritual Deception

> "Does the Lord delight in burnt offerings and sacrifices as much as in obeying the Lord? To obey is better than sacrifice, and to heed is better than the fat of rams. For rebellion is like the sin of divination and arrogance like the evil of idolatry. Because you have rejected the word of the Lord, He will also reject you." (1 Samuel 15:22-23)

After what I began calling my own Damascus Road experience, I started to attend church on a regular basis. For a short season I attended the Pentecostal Church, as that was where God found me. However, I soon discovered that in spite of all its graces and focus on the Holy Spirit, it was not the church for me. My new friends, who had taken me to that first service, were not members; in fact, they were part of the United Church of Canada, but they spent a lot of time in fellowship and study with a small charismatic group that met in the United Church on Sunday nights. This group loved and cared for me; God used them to bring some healing and stability into my life, and here is where I began to grow in my faith. Unfortunately, it was this small group that in many ways also wreaked tremendous havoc in my life. As a result of some of the advice that came from one particular leader, I suffered severely from the life-changing decisions she encouraged me to make. Some in the group also blindly followed her manipulations.

After I joined the church, my daily prayer was that I would be reconciled with Doreen and that our marriage would be restored. Day after day that was my prayer. From reading Scripture I discovered that divorce does not please God. I so badly wanted reconciliation with Doreen and to raise her expected child as our own. But Doreen definitely did not want reconciliation—in fact, after I came to Christ she didn't want anything more to do with me. Once she had the baby I never saw her again. To this day I do not know if, in the end, she married Bill. All I could do was pray for her peace and ask the Lord to bless her and her family. By God's grace I carry no animosity towards Bill or Doreen.

Among the young people who attended the evening service in the United Church, several were divorced or single. Most were relatively new Christians, but what we had in common was that we were all seeking God's perfect will for our lives. We met, prayed, and worshipped together with that one goal in mind. What did God want us to do with the rest of our lives?

One evening at the church service, I met Elizabeth. She was a young and beautiful woman with extremely sad eyes and a beautiful singing voice. Immediately after we met, some in the group began encouraging Elizabeth and me to begin a relationship. At the time, I was not really interested in a relationship, as I had just come through a divorce. But Elizabeth and I met on a Sunday evening, and by Tuesday people were talking about us becoming engaged! A key leader of this charismatic group was

Alice Clarke, the main proponent of this suggestion. To this day Alice Clarke remains a conundrum to me. When I met Elizabeth, Alice was very involved in Elizabeth's life. I thought Alice was a spiritual giant as she appeared to have a deep, meaningful relationship with God. I was in awe of her and it was not difficult for her to take me under her wing. I had just come to Christ, my first marriage had ended in disaster, and I was extremely vulnerable. I was desperate for love and affection. Alice was convinced and in turn convinced us and the others that God had selected Elizabeth and me for each other and that there was no question that it was His will for our lives. To both Elizabeth and me, it seemed very hurried and quite overwhelming. We did not know each other, but the majority of the group all agreed that it was a great idea. In time, we also got caught up with excitement at the idea that Almighty God had taken such an interest in our lives and that he would draw us together so quickly. The way we saw it, God thought we were so special that He would personally arrange our marriage!

I was not sure that this was how God worked, but those with more spiritual experience said it was quite normal. In my ignorance, and out of a desperate desire to be special, I ignored all the red flags that were waving in my face and, in retrospect, were so obvious. You may ask, *How could he have been so naïve?* But naïve is not the word that I use when I think back to this time in my life. Instead, words such as *stupid*, *foolish*, *irresponsible*, and *rash* come to mind. If you had asked me back in 1981, "How could you be so naïve?" I would not have had an answer for you. But when I look back now, I can offer two explanations: First, I didn't have anyone that I could honestly talk to. My parents were out of the question, and the friends in the group were too caught up in the group themselves to offer any concrete advice. I had absolutely no one that I could go to for counsel. Second,

I was so in need of love and so desperate to be accepted and to be somebody that I was blind. For most of my life, my will had been manipulated and controlled by others, and I honestly did not know that I had a free will. Believe it or not, I did not know that God gave us a free will and that we all have the right to choose. At that time I honestly did not realize that I could choose to marry Elizabeth or choose not to marry Elizabeth. Why did I not know that?

Thirty-six years later I do have an answer: As the charismatic movement grew in the churches, in the late seventies and early eighties, a new form of "shepherding" emerged. This gave authority to lay leaders over new disciples coming into the church. Sometimes these lay leaders were called "under-shepherds" to the pastor, and their responsibility was to teach new disciples how to grow in their faith. At least that is the role Alice took in the lives of Elizabeth and me. Looking back now, I recognize that some of her teachings were perverse, unbiblical, and required almost strict obedience to her. It was a time of unquestioning loyalty and obedience to those in authority. Having been raised in a military family, and serving in the military at the time I began to attend church, I was a prime target for this kind of spiritual manipulation.

I now understand that it is a parent's responsibility to affirm the personhood of their children. If they do not, the children will look to others to affirm that personhood. Consequently, they eventually become totally dependent on those leaders and they are willing to do almost anything to win their approval. However, they also fear the punishment that will come if they disobey the leaders. If they are disobedient, they risk being ostracized and rejected. Being banished by those in the group was not the biggest threat; it was the threat of being shunned by God for wilful disobedience to what others perceived to be

His will for our lives. During my formative years I certainly did not have the love and support of a mother, and so when Alice offered me these things I easily succumbed. I confess now that she completely dominated Elizabeth and me, as we were starving for approval from a parental figure. When I look back, I realize that I looked upon Alice as a bit of a goddess, and today I can say with certainty that she totally bewitched me. Why she chose us to be the recipients of her affections and gifts remains another one of life's mysteries. Part of the answer may be that Alice was using me to unburden herself of the heavy load she carried in nurturing Elizabeth.

In 1981, I desperately needed to be loved, and the idea that God had personally selected my wife for me made me, I thought, a super-spiritual giant in His eyes and in the eyes of others. Furthermore, I believed if God selected my wife, then this marriage would not end in divorce. After all, how many other marriages had God personally arranged? Looking back, I feel shame and tremendous regret for the pain and sorrow that I brought on myself and Elizabeth. At the same time that I didn't want to be married, Elizabeth did not want to marry me. I wasn't the kind of husband she'd imagined. Of the two of us, I was the stronger one, and I so regret allowing others to make decisions on our behalf. God has healed the pain and forgiven the sin, but I still wonder what could have been if the two of us had had the courage of our convictions and walked away from this arranged marriage. I wonder how I could have been so blind and allowed myself to be led so far astray. The cry of my heart from 1981 until today is still the same: *Lord Jesus Christ, Son of the Living God, have mercy on me, a sinner.*

Shortly after Elizabeth and I met, I was once again posted to Camp Borden for another course, leading to my promotion as sergeant. While I was at Camp Borden, the mail again became my friend, but I quickly discovered that Elizabeth was not a letter-writer and that we would not get to know each other through correspondence. In the few letters she wrote, it was obvious that she was an extremely frightened woman and that she had a hard time maintaining relationships. Every event in those days was spiritualized, and so when Elizabeth told me she was hearing voices telling her to harm herself, I dismissed them as being from the devil as that is what others told me. I had no idea that she was ill or how ill she really was. She had no close family or friends. When she made friends she somehow quickly lost them. Did I miss the red flags? No, I totally ignored the red flags. In my ignorance and arrogance I thought I could be Elizabeth's saviour. I thought if I could love her, it would drive away the voices and all her fears, and I would be her knight in shining armour. How foolish of me!

On my return from Camp Borden in December, I discovered that all the wedding plans had been made and that we were to be married the following April. That caused me to panic, and for a brief moment the lights went on as I suddenly began to realize what I was getting myself into. I was overwhelmed as it was all happening far too quickly. I had to put the brakes on this fast-moving train. Both Elizabeth and I did our best to stop the runaway express, but we failed. We were not strong enough to stand up to Alice and her manipulative ways. We didn't have the resources within ourselves to stand against what I would now call wicked behaviour.

In January 1981, we sat down with Alice and one of her prayer partners, and we tried to talk our way out of the marriage. We wanted all the plans to be cancelled. Elizabeth and I had spent time together and realized we did not know each other well enough to be married. We were not even sure that we were compatible. We thought we should have more time with each other before taking this major step. We were trying to be responsible adults and take ownership of our lives and our walk with God. During our meeting with Alice and her prayer partner, we were told in no uncertain terms that if we did not get married in April, we were in direct rebellion against God and His will for our lives. The Scripture to which we were directed was taken from the First Book of Samuel, referring to the consequences for King Saul when he deliberately disobeyed the Prophet Samuel. Samuel said to Saul, "Rebellion is like the sin of witchcraft and arrogance like the evil of idolatry. Because you have rejected the word of the Lord, He will also reject you . . ."[12] We were told that if we did not marry in April, we would be banished from the family of God. We would be forsaken by Him and never again know His presence and His peace.

As my parents knew that I was now attending a Protestant church, I was virtually banished from my biological family; I certainly did not want to be banished from God's family. Lost and insecure as we were, the threat of such action was extremely harsh and cruel. I had only begun my walk with Jesus less than two years before, and the prospect of banishment from God's family was too much for me. I was forcefully told again and again: God is telling you to marry and to care for Elizabeth. I was told if I wanted to be in God's will, this was now my primary responsibility in life. I had no idea then that people would use Scripture to manipulate and intimidate others. I did not know that Scripture must be interpreted in light of Scripture. In other words, Scripture is interpreted in the context of all Scriptures. I did not know that God never rushes His children into life-changing decisions.

It is said that the love of God is the greatest gift that He has given to this world. I believe that although love is an absolutely

12 1 Samuel 15:23

amazing gift of God, and we cannot live without it, His most amazing gift is the gift of free will to every person. God never robs us of this, and I do not believe that He ever forces us into decisions against our beliefs. He expects obedience from us, but He never forces His will upon us.

I decided to go and see my parents prior to the wedding. Although we lived in the same city, after I left home, I did not make a habit of visiting them, as I had been told by my siblings that they were extremely upset that I had left the Catholic Church. I justified not going to see them as it would stir up further dissension in our already fragile relationship. However, I knew I needed to make the effort now, especially since I was to be married again. I wore my dress uniform with my new sergeant stripes proudly displayed. I thought surely they would be impressed that after only six years I was a sergeant, four years ahead of my peers. But there were no words of recognition or congratulations. I think that was the moment the penny finally dropped. I realized that no matter what I did, I would never win my parents' approval. I think that was my last effort to try and win their love and acceptance. During this visit I decided I would have a serious talk with my mother, as I felt a great deal of animosity towards her. While we sat in the living room, I asked if we could talk about my childhood. She immediately stood up and walked out of the room, muttering, "You were a difficult child." That was the end of the conversation. On that visit I did not mention the subject of my upcoming marriage.

I returned a couple of weeks later and told them that I was getting married in April. They were furious because I had no intention of having my marriage to Doreen annulled in the Catholic Church. My mother read all the tabloids you see at the checkout counters at the grocery store. She showed me a story in one of those papers about some world-famous person who got an annulment after twenty-eight years of marriage and four children. Getting an annulment seemed to me to be the most ridiculous exercise possible. How could the Catholic Church say that after twenty-eight years of marriage and four children the marriage could be annulled? My marriage to Doreen had been a real marriage, and I could not in good conscience apply for it to be annulled. To me annulment smacks of hypocrisy and clearly shows a lack of integrity. My marriage had failed, and just because they thought I had grounds to get an annulment, it did not mean that I should get one.

After meeting with my parents, I thought it would be prudent to meet and talk with my father alone. As I mentioned to you in the prologue, I only remember having one meaningful conversation with my father, and when it took place, it did not go very well. I invited him out for breakfast and a game of golf. I was twenty-eight years old and this was the very first occasion I can remember spending time alone with my father. After nine holes of golf, we went to breakfast, and I asked for his blessing if I was to marry again. It did not go well. He told me in no uncertain terms that if I married a second time, I would be disowned as I would have to get married outside the Catholic Church. Until then I did not think it was possible for a parent to completely disown their child. In my parents' eyes, leaving the Catholic Church was the gravest sin I could commit. Except for two very brief encounters, I would not see my father again for seven years.

And so I prepared for my marriage to Elizabeth, despite our very serious reservations. I walked down the aisle with a sense of heaviness and fear instead of joy and celebration. As a Christian I was still far too immature and lacked the courage to stand up to the spiritual manipulation that was taking place. From the moment we exchanged our marriage vows until fourteen years later when it was dissolved, it was an absolute and total catastrophe. While we were on our honeymoon, Elizabeth finally told me her history. I learned that her father had robbed a bank and died in Kingston Penitentiary; she had no brothers or sisters and was estranged from her mother. Her grandmother had raised her. She had never worked and she collected a disability allowance from the government, which stopped after we were married. At the time I did not know this disability allowance was based on the fact that Elizabeth had been previously diagnosed with mental illness.

I am confident to this day that Alice had cautioned Elizabeth not to tell me her life story until after we were married. Also, on our honeymoon, Elizabeth told me that she had spent most of her life in and out of Ottawa's mental hospital. She had undergone numerous electroconvulsive therapies (electric shock treatments) and years earlier she had been diagnosed as paranoid schizophrenic. At the time I had no idea what that medical term meant. I could understand cancer, strokes, and heart attacks, but mental illness was truly beyond my grasp. I did not know that those who have been diagnosed with paranoid schizophrenia are often delusional. Nor did I know that some suffer from hallucinations and others hear voices, if they do not remain on their prescribed medication. When these things began to manifest themselves in our marriage, it frightened me as I did not know how to fix them. I had no idea what lay ahead. Shortly before we were married, Alice had convinced Elizabeth to throw out all her medications. I didn't even know she had been taking medication. Elizabeth had been told by Alice that once she was married, by faith she was healed. She had been manipulated into believing that all she needed to be healed was to have faith and to be loved. I knew nothing about this until after we were married.

I discovered early in our marriage that Elizabeth seemed to be incapable of loving others or receiving love. She lived in a paranoid world filled with fantasy where one day she would act like an adult and the next like a giddy teenager or a petulant child. She was not able to maintain a home or hold a job. She was barely capable of consummating our marriage. She suffered from persecutory delusions and constantly had the compulsion to harm herself. Her paranoia was constant, and a week after our marriage, we began consulting counsellors in the hope of helping her get well. I lost count of the number of counsellors, doctors, and therapists we saw in the fourteen years of our marriage, hoping that someone would be able to help her find peace of mind. Because of Elizabeth's paranoia, she could not sustain relationships. Women were a threat to her and she would enter into fantasy relationships with my male friends. She was constantly looking for a father figure and the perfect prince who would sweep her off her feet. During our marriage, I recall only one or two genuine friendships that she could call her own.

My yearly journals disclose the sadness, struggles, frustrations and disappointments we lived through during our fourteen years of marriage. But the bottom line was that Elizabeth was sick. Unless one maintains a strict regime of medications and counselling, it is impossible for someone with paranoid schizophrenia to live a stable life. I do not hold Elizabeth responsible for the failure of our marriage. The situation for both of us was impossible. Elizabeth needed to be on constant medication and under the direct care of physicians and psychiatrists. But she was not and, consequently, she suffered horribly from hallucinations, delusions, and paranoid fantasies. I am a person of faith and live in a world of faith, but I have yet to see anyone healed of this particular disease by the laying on of hands, the anointing with oil, or the sprinkling of holy water to make them well. Although

I believe in miracles, I also believe in doctors, nurses, medicine and therapy. These are also gifts used by God to heal the sick.

Looking back on the years in Ottawa as members of that charismatic group, I can see that we allowed Alice to have far too much control over our lives. Upon reflection as a mature Christian, I have no doubt that we were being spiritually abused in the worst way possible and what happened to us was evil. We were both asked to do something that we did not choose to do; furthermore, we were not capable of bearing that burden. The burden of responsibility for Elizabeth's care was far beyond what I was equipped to handle. I had absolutely no idea how to properly care for her.

After we were married, my relationship with Elizabeth was such a massive shock to me that I met with Alice again to try to understand what I had become involved in. She promised to help me and teach me how to care for Elizabeth. She said it was now my primary task in life. She also told us that God had told her to spiritually adopt us as her children. I would have a new family, including a younger brother and sister. In order to complete this spiritual adoption, it would be necessary for me to legally change my name. You may not understand this. You may see it as absolute foolishness and think that anyone should have been able to see through it. But I could not. Since my father had disowned me and I was no longer in relationship with most of my family, Alice believed that, acting on the Lord's behalf, she would receive us into her family. The Scripture that was used to justify this adoption was from Psalm 27: "Though my father and mother forsake me, the Lord will receive me."[13] Since I had so many wounds and was so desperate to be loved, the idea of belonging to a family who would love me and not disown me was of the utmost importance to me. Again, at the time I was

13 Psalm 27:10

not able to discern the spiritual manipulation in this. So we went through the legal process to change our names, and overnight we became Ronald and Elizabeth Clarke. Oh, the foolish things we do in an effort to be loved, to belong, and to be accepted.

Looking back, changing my family name was probably one of the harshest things I could have done in striking back at my parents for their lack of affection and love. Even though the idea was not mine, by legally changing my name I was effectively saying, "If you disown me, I in turn will disown you." In other words, the way I could hurt them most and strike back at my father was to give up the family name. I do not know if I was subconsciously trying to wound my earthly father or whether I trying to find a family who would love me, which was all I ever wanted.

Although we had entered into a disastrous marriage, I still held fast to the idea that God had told us to marry each other. I often said to others that God told us to do it. Day after day my heart was in anguish, and I was overwhelmed wondering what the future would hold for us.

To be absolutely fair to Elizabeth, it was just as much of a struggle for her. I was the wrong man for her and she definitely did not want to be married to me. I thought that I had endured my fair share of life's burdens, and I hoped for a marriage of joy and peace and eventually children and grandchildren. It seemed that when I looked for good, evil came, and when I looked for light, I was overwhelmed with darkness. The churning inside me never stopped, and I think as a result of the stress of those years, I began to encounter heart problems in my early forties. *God told us to marry each other* became the mantra I repeated for fourteen long years.

CHAPTER TEN
The Future Unfolds

"The Spirit of the Lord is on me, because He has anointed me to proclaim good news to the poor. He has sent me to proclaim freedom for the prisoners and recovery of sight for the blind, to set the oppressed free and proclaim the year of the Lord's favour." (Luke 4:18–19)

The most positive thing that came from the charismatic group was the Scripture verse quoted above. One of the ladies from the group (not Alice) called one night and told me God had laid these words for my future on her heart. I knew this woman was not a manipulator, but had, in my opinion, also been manipulated into a very unhealthy marriage. This particular word of prophecy resonated with my spirit; I knew it was a genuine word from the Lord, and in His time He would bring it to pass. I was content to wait on his timing.

Four years into our marriage, I left the military as I felt that God was calling me to full-time Christian ministry. I had no idea what kind of ministry it was to be. The desire of my heart that I received on the night of my conversion had never left me and I wanted to proclaim the Gospel. The Ottawa group did not want us to leave, but I felt that God was calling, and this time I acted on the courage of my convictions. I knew with certainty that we needed to be out from under Alice's influence, and this separation was the best thing that could have happened to us. We moved to the Eastern Townships of Quebec, where I became the assistant director of Quebec Lodge, which was an Anglican camp. It was there I received my call to join the Anglican Church. In my earlier book, *The Bishop or the King*, I relate my conversion to Anglicanism and the beginning of my life and ministry in the Anglican Church of Canada. It is worth repeating here for those who have not read that story:

> Never for a moment did I think that God would call me into full-time ministry or into the priesthood of the Anglican Church, but indeed He did. In 1983, I left the military and moved to the Eastern Townships of Quebec, near Montreal, where I helped rebuild an Anglican summer camp. I had spent the previous summer at Quebec Lodge as a camp counsellor and they invited me back as a member of their full-time staff. I knew that to work at the camp full-time was a call from God, but I had no idea of God's long-range plans. My intention was to spend a year at Quebec Lodge praying and seeking God's will for my life. I thought that when the year was over I would move on to something else, but certainly not into any kind of full-time Anglican

ministry or seminary. But it was at Quebec Lodge that I was found by Anglicanism.

One Friday night, a colleague from the camp asked if I would be willing to go to a local church on Sunday morning and lead them through Morning Prayer. I didn't know what Morning Prayer was, and so he gave me a copy of the 1962 *Book of Common Prayer*. As I began to read the book, I asked him if people really prayed this way, using the King James language of 'thee and thou.' He told me yes, millions of Anglicans the world over prayed this way. I thought it was a strange way to pray, but I got really excited when I looked through the Morning Prayer service and came across the rubric, which stated: 'A sermon may be preached here . . .'[14] Once I discovered that I could preach about Jesus, I was more than willing to lead Morning Prayer. I could certainly work my way through these strange prayers in an ancient language if I had the opportunity to preach. I soon discovered that the Book of Common Prayer is a solid book of Scriptural prayers and daily offices, which uplifts and nurtures my soul to this day, both in my private and public worship.

When I went to lead Morning Prayer that first Sunday morning, there were eight people in the church. I spent the rest of that year at that

14 *Book of Common Prayer* (Toronto: Anglican Book Center, 1962), 15. Henceforth, BCP.

> church, Sunday after Sunday, leading Morning Prayer and preaching the Gospel. Those eight people invited their friends and family members, and soon the congregation grew to over fifty. It was these humble, uncomplicated people in that little mining town of Eustis, Quebec, who first told me that I should go to seminary and become an Anglican priest. I spent a second year in the Eastern Townships of Quebec working with the local parish priest in a three-point charge, examining Anglicanism and testing the legitimacy of my call.[15]

I started my Theology studies at Bishop's University in Lennoxville, Quebec, and in the fall of 1985 we moved to Montreal. There I attended Montreal Theological College, and in June of 1987 I was ordained and assigned a curacy at St. Stephen's Church in Westmount, Quebec. While we were in Montreal, we received a phone call from Alice telling us that God told her to break off communications with us. So much for my new adopted family! But by that time, I was standing on my own two feet and starting to become the person that I believe God intended me to be.

My curacy in Montreal was absolutely wonderful, although wonderful is not a big enough word to describe my two years at St. Stephen's. I worked in a glorious partnership with the rector; and St. Stephen's was a parish in which I could do no wrong. I was loved, appreciated, and trained to one day become a rector of a parish myself. I had a bishop who prayed for me, supported me, and took time monthly to meet with all the curates in the diocese as part of our training. I had numerous godly mentors

15 Ron Corcoran, *The Bishop or the King*, pp. 24–25.

who helped me adjust to ministry life. If I had known what the future would hold, I believe I would have stayed in Montreal, but I was itching to make my mark in the world of ministry. At this stage in my life, I still had not lost the foolish ambition to be someone! If I could be someone, maybe my family would hear about it and finally love me the way that I desperately needed. Several months after my ordination, my world was once again turned upside down.

In October of 1987, I received the dreaded phone call that I knew would eventually come. My sister Annie told me that our father had died and asked if I would come home for the funeral. It had been almost seven years since I had seen many members of my family, and again I was faced with an extremely difficult decision. If I did not go home, I knew that I would probably never see any of my family members again; but then I thought that if I *did* go home, it could be the start of healing and reconciliation with my siblings and possibly with my mother. In boldness and optimism, I chose to go. I went to Ottawa by myself as I did not want Elizabeth to have to deal with the stress of the funeral and being with my family. The only person that I had seen in the past seven years was my brother Joseph, as he was studying at the same university I was. When I went home it was extremely difficult, and I felt like a stranger in the midst of my family members. I sensed I was seen as the black sheep, and I only stayed in Ottawa one night with one of my older brothers. I raced back to Montreal almost immediately after the service.

When I finally arrived at the funeral home, I went to the open coffin and looked down at my father. Although I was thirty-five years old, I felt like a child once again. A flood of fear coursed through my body, simply because I was standing right next to him, and I realized anew just how frightened I had been of him my entire life. I looked at him lying there and thought, *I no longer have to fear you.* Even as a grown man I still felt shame, and had a sense for how I carried within me so much sorrow and disappointment. As it had been when he was alive, I did not know what to say to my father—nor did I know what to say to my siblings. I felt like a stranger in their midst.

The next day at the funeral service, I was determined to remain as stoic as possible and I almost succeeded. I had not reckoned, however, on God's intervention. When we came to the words in the Lord's Prayer, *Forgive us our trespasses as we forgive those who trespass against us,* I became very emotional and began to weep and could not stop. All the years of repressed frustrations and regrets began to flow, not in words of anger, but in tears, abundant and uncontrollable. I wept for all the losses we had both endured. My weeping was muffled but audible, but no-one came near to comfort me. Although I was surrounded by family, once again I found myself alone.

After the service, I went to stand on the steps outside the church to try to pull myself together. It was a cold October day and the wind was howling. I looked up to heaven, and I said to God, "All I wanted was a father I could be in relationship with—a *real* relationship. I wanted to know my father." At that moment the wind died down, and in my heart I clearly heard God say to me, *Someday you will.* To this day, I don't know if the Spirit was speaking to me about knowing my earthly father or my Heavenly Father. It doesn't make that much difference, but I know at that very moment, I was reconciled and at peace with my father. Yes, my father's funeral was another turning point in my life as the process for reconciliation began that very day. Today my relationships with my family members have been completely restored.

I returned to Montreal after the funeral, and a year later I accepted the position of associate pastor in a church in downtown Vancouver, British Columbia. How did this come about? I now confess that my arrogance and my hunger to be someone raised its ugly head once again. To this day, I do not know whether I went to Vancouver because God called me, or if I went on my own volition, or if I was manipulated into going. It could have been a combination of all three. A well-known Anglican British evangelist had come to Montreal to lead an evangelism conference. While there, he told the local clergy he was seeking someone who would work with him to, as he said, save "hedonistic" Vancouver. They recommended me as having a passion to tell others about Christ and that I had the gift of evangelism, but it needed to be refined. I agreed to go. When I first contemplated ministry it wasn't only church ministry, but evangelism and healing ministries, that stirred the passion in my soul. I confess that it was pretty intoxicating to be 'head-hunted' by this evangelist and chosen especially to work with him. He promised that I would be equipped and would have the opportunity to lead evangelistic missions across the country. This was my opportunity, and I would be known and recognized by others as his protégé.

That did not happen. In fact, in the four years we spent together, I did one mission outreach with him, and that took place in Vancouver North. Looking back, I was still extremely naïve—I assumed that those who invite you to do a task will equip you and stand with you in good times and in bad. It was not completely his fault that when I arrived in Vancouver, the bottom fell out of my hopes and dreams of ever being an evangelist.

Vancouver was to be my Waterloo—the absolute total breaking point of my life.

CHAPTER ELEVEN
Disaster Strikes

"So if you think you are standing firm, be careful that you do not fall. No temptation has overtaken you except what is common to mankind. And God is faithful; He will not let you be tempted beyond what you can bear. But when you are tempted, He will also provide a way out so that you can endure it." (1 Corinthians 10:12-13)

Trust me, I fell. On August 30, 1989 we moved to Vancouver, British Columbia, where I was to become the associate priest of Holy Trinity Anglican Church and to evangelize with my British counterpart. We arrived and spent the night with the parish rector. The next day, after showing us a house we could possibly rent, he asked me to drop him off at the Synod office as the bishop wanted to meet with him. I was to return to his apartment in the early afternoon to arrange for a phone for our new residence. When I returned, he was not there. So I drove around for a while and then parked the car and went up to his apartment a second time. When he opened the door, he was as white as a sheet. He told me that he had been dismissed by the Diocese and closed the door. In bewilderment I called the Synod office and was told I could not see the bishop until after Thanksgiving, and the archdeacon of the Diocese would be at Holy Trinity on Sunday morning. On Sunday the archdeacon told the congregation that he had come to share good news and bad news.

The good news was that their new associate priest had arrived and was on staff. The bad news was that the rector had been dismissed for inappropriate behaviour with a parishioner. That was the end of his statement and no further details were given. He left immediately after the service. The British evangelist who was the catalyst in my coming to Vancouver was on vacation. So following the service, the congregation turned to me as their new associate priest, wanting to know what had happened. Was the previous rector having an affair with a parishioner? Were their children in any kind of danger? I had as much information as they did, and I had no way to ease their fears. I didn't know it at the time, but the bishop and the Diocesan staff were in conflict with the parish, and that is why I could not get the information I needed in order to respond in an appropriate manner. Needless to say, it wasn't much of a welcome to the West Coast!

The parish now had no rector, but eventually I was appointed, and the first two years were fairly good. Regretfully, I had to set aside my hopes and dreams of being trained as an evangelist as the needs of the parish were overwhelming and I did not have time to do mission work and run a parish at the same time. The parish work was extremely hard work because we had the clergy failure *and* we were in the process of finding a site and building a five-million-dollar structure. Although those first two years were difficult, I felt that, in time, the whole congregation would be able to move ahead as a unified organization. In 1991, I was invited to do a pulpit exchange with a parish in Birmingham, England. Their rector was to come to Vancouver and teach on the gifts of the Spirit, and I was to go to Christ Church Birmingham and teach on evangelism. But while I was gone, something in the parish changed. When I came back, the parish was in chaos. I have often wondered if it had something to do with the fact that I was not present when one of our very popular parishioners died. There was a young couple in the parish who had recently married and had a new baby, and life was perfect for the three of them. One day, while playing soccer, the husband collapsed and was rushed to hospital. While doing tests, the doctors found a very fast-moving cancer, and within two months he was dead. I was not present when he died. Did people think that I should not have been overseas when this happened? I don't know if that was the reason for the chaos, but it was certainly chaotic when I returned at the end of August. By mid-September I felt that everything that I had worked for in the first two years had unravelled.

When crises occur in parishes, as in any other organization, people tend to break off into splinter groups, some in agreement with whatever is happening and others against. Consequently, the things that are hidden in the darkness start to come into the light, and if they are not managed well, it can destroy a community. I confess that I did not manage it well. A parish meeting in October exposed many of the weaknesses of the parish, and when that meeting was over, the majority of the leadership resigned. I was far too insecure and, unlike in Montreal, I did not have mentors in place, nor did I have a bishop who I felt I could trust to help me keep my head above water.

Over a period of time, I discovered that the congregation was more or less split into six different factions. First, there were those who were dyed-in-the-wool Anglicans. For the most part they did not want anything in the parish to change. Some had been parishioners for over forty or fifty years, and they were quite content to attend their weekly services, host their teas, and eventually be buried from the church. After all, this was their church, it was their parents' church and, for some, their grandparents' church.

The second group comprised those who resented the newcomers who had come into their parish, and who they believed had sold their building out from underneath them. Consequently, the parish found themselves in the middle of a five-million-dollar building project they did not want. They were quite content to stay at their current location, not thinking about the needs of future generations of Anglicans. They, too, considered it their church and resented these young whippersnappers who had come in and turned their lives upside down.

The third group was made up of those who were associated with a local Christian college and thought that clergy should play a minor role in the parish, and that laity should have the overall responsibility for the daily life of the parish. In other words, it was hinted to me on a number of occasions that the clergy should be seen and not heard. This was completely contrary to my training in seminary and in my curacy in Montreal. In my military career and church career, I had always been a hands-on leader, but I am also a very capable delegator. That is my personality, and that is the way I was trained. I was anxious to be involved in the day-to-day operations of a parish and to get others to participate with me. I did not understand the new concept of leading from the rear. This faction accused me of trying to take over the parish, and it may have appeared that way to some. But all I wanted was to serve God to the best of my ability.

The fourth group were newcomers to the parish who had joined the church as a result of encouragement from the English Evangelist. Previously, they had been an independent church and the leadership had been provided by the laity. These people had been led to believe that after five years, the parish would be able to separate from the Diocese and have nothing to do with the Anglican governance system. I became aware that there were a fair number of parishioners who were anti-clergy and anti-diocese. For those who are not familiar with the Anglican Church, the system of a diocese is the way the church supports and upholds the parishes in each geographical area. When I was first told that the church was going to break with the Diocese, I did not believe that anyone would ever say something like that publicly. I later discovered correspondence from the former rector clearly stating that disassociation from the Diocese and Anglicanism was part of the long-term future plans of the parish.

Fifth, there was a group that is found in every parish: people who are there to have their personal needs met and who expect the clergy to meet each and every one of those needs. For the most part, they sit on the sidelines and do not actively participate in the life of the parish, but are often ready to offer all kinds of criticism.

Finally, there was a small group of people who were extremely supportive, but these were few in number, especially after our disastrous public meeting. Only two years into my ordination, I was ill-equipped to deal with all the chaos that I discovered when I returned from England. My well-known and world-renowned British evangelist, who was attached to the parish, often spoke publicly and was very critical of the Diocese and the Canadian House of Bishops. And so I had very little support from the Diocese and the clergy. I had no idea how to deal with a parish in which there was so much dissension. One person who was my constant source of encouragement was the Rev. Dr. Harry Robinson, the rector of St. John's Church in Shaughnessy. He helped me through some of my darkest days, but I confess the parish broke me in soul and spirit.

I readily admit that I did not have the experience or the life skills to deal with the situation in the parish. I do take full responsibility for the catastrophes that took place under my leadership. Inexperienced as I was, there was far too much pressure for me to succeed. It is difficult enough being a pastor of a parish, but being a pastor of a parish that is so full of dissension and involved in building a new facility was more than I could handle.

Admittedly, there were some very good things that took place in the parish. People made first-time commitments to Christ, couples were married, babies were baptized, and teenagers were confirmed. Bible study groups were formed and people were sent off to the mission field. Some couples formed relationships that carry on to this day. The church is still in existence, but I am not sure how many of the people who were there when I was the rector are currently active members of the church. However, right from the beginning of my tenure at Holy Trinity I was for the most part lost, but in the fall of 1991 my ministry at the parish took a terrible turn from which I never recovered. I spiralled downward into a severe depression. In the midst of all that was going on, my relationship with God suffered greatly. I lost Him for a season and it took a long time to rebuild my trust in His plan and provision for my life.

I do want you to know that Elizabeth, in spite of her sickness, did all she could do to stand with me during this difficult time in the parish. She tried as hard as she could to be a supportive pastor's wife during this period, but this turmoil certainly did not help the two of us. With all this going on, I had very little time to devote to my sick wife, and our marriage began to show clear signs of disintegration. It was at this time my role in the marriage changed, in that I had to move from protecting her to functioning for her. I confess that in many ways I withdrew. During our years in Ottawa, Montreal, and Vancouver we saw numerous counsellors, therapists, and doctors. I clung desperately to the hope that someone would be able to help. Elizabeth would not stay on her medications, and I had reached my limit trying to help her. Over time I had become very frightened of Elizabeth. Her mental illness and emotional instability really scared me. My marriage was very much like reliving my childhood. I was petrified to come home from work, not knowing what I would find or what new crisis I would have to deal with. Waking up in the morning and going to sleep at night frightened me, so I lived in a state of constant fear. It was emotionally draining. I know now that those who have been abused often wrestle with tiredness and are weary all the time, because they failed to live up to others' expectations. I had been spiritually abused in having been coerced into marriage, and I could not fix myself or Elizabeth. Since I could not live up to the expectations placed on me by myself and others while in Vancouver, I felt as though I was being abused all over again. I was bone weary!

While we were in England in the summer of 1991, we travelled to a healing school called Ellel Grange. This school is located in Lancaster, England, and we attended a week-long healing retreat. This retreat gave us the opportunity to be ministered to individually and as a couple. I knew in my heart when we went that this was one more desperate attempt to heal a marriage that from the very beginning was set for failure. During one of our counselling sessions, one of the mysteries in our marriage was finally revealed. Elizabeth explained that in the week after our wedding, Alice made her dress in her wedding gown and had brought her back to the church where we were married. Alice then took Elizabeth through a second wedding ceremony, but this time she was married to Christ. Alice told Elizabeth that Christ was now her true husband. She was told that the only time we were allowed to be intimate was when we were both under the anointing of the Holy Spirit. Sworn to secrecy, Elizabeth kept that secret for twelve years. She was further told that if we were intimate without being under the anointing of the Holy Spirit, any children we conceived would be children of the devil. From our honeymoon onward there was no real sexual or emotional intimacy between us. Elizabeth was absolutely terrified of sexual intimacy. I knew in a loving and healthy marriage, one partner should never force themselves upon the other, so that part of our lives was shut down completely.

I was shocked when I found out about this so-called second marriage, but I then understood the absence of intimacy and the fact that we had no children. I had always wanted children of my own to love, nurture, and raise to be secure, compassionate adults. Alice and Elizabeth knew how desperately I wanted to be a father, but with the foolishness that we went through in this arranged marriage those dreams had to be permanently set aside. Initially, I was not sure that Elizabeth's story about the second marriage was the truth, because she was proficient at weaving elaborate tales. That is not to say Elizabeth was a compulsive liar, but she lived largely in a delusional and paranoid world.

A number of years later I met other couples from the Ottawa group, and some told me that they had also participated in a second wedding. I believe the purpose of the second wedding was to draw the couples closer to Jesus, but it was totally without merit. This happens in charismatic groups that deviate from Scripture and grounded theology. To understand this kind of spiritual manipulation I recommend a book called *Possessing The*

Gates of the Enemy: A Training Manual for Militant Intercession, by Cindy Jacobs.[16] Chapter Ten, "Flaky Intercession," provides the best information I have read about speaking words of (so-called) knowledge or direction into other people's lives. The author does the Body of Christ a major service as she also covers the Bridal Chamber. She indicates she hesitated to write about this, but I am grateful she did. She writes of those who have this *special intimate* relationship with Christ that others do not have. When you have a special intimate relationship with Christ, you are invited into what is called the Bridal Chamber with Christ. This kind of theology is called Gnosticism, and has been around since the second century.[17] It is secret knowledge restricted to those in the know. The Apostles Paul and John addressed Gnosticism in their Epistles, Paul in The Epistle to the Galatians, and John in Epistles that bear his name. I believe that those who lead people astray in this fashion are guilty of gross theological spiritual abuse. The effects of that abuse can linger in peoples' lives for decades. A strong person, secure within herself or himself and not battling mental illness, might be able to sort through what being married to Jesus really means. After all, the Church is called the Bride of Christ.[18] Someone who has been diagnosed as paranoid schizophrenic is utterly defenceless against such spiritual abuse and manipulation. Elizabeth and I were grievously sinned against by this spiritual leader.

In Vancouver, I finally realized that I did not have the resources to provide Elizabeth with the help she required. Once again I began setting up appointments with another counsellor. Yet again I sought to end the pain and anguish we

16 Cindy Jacobs, *Possessing The Gates of the Enemy — Third Edition, Revised with Study Guide* (Chosen Books, 2009) Pages 119–136

17 Wkipedia.org/wike/Gnosticism

18 Revelation 19:7

suffered. Although the primary focus had always been on helping Elizabeth, I recognized that I was on the verge of a complete breakdown and needed help myself. I was almost forty years old and my life was a complete disaster. The ministry that I was so sure God had called me into was also an utter disaster. I reached out one more time. The person we met was Dr. Becca Johnson, and she was a registered psychologist in B.C. and had a counselling practice at a local Baptist church. She was not encouraging about the future of our marriage, but she was willing to work with each of us on our histories. This was another turning point in my life.

CHAPTER TWELVE
Once Again, Redemption

"My soul thirsts for God, for the Living God. When can I go and meet with God? My tears have been my food day and night, while people say to me all day long, Where is your God . . . Why, my soul, are you downcast? Why so disturbed within me? Put your hope in God, for I will yet praise Him, my Saviour and my God." (Psalm 42: 2–3, 11)

As I outlined in the previous chapter, in the summer of 1991, I did an exchange in Birmingham, England. When I returned that fall, I found the parish in chaos. It seemed that the parish, the diocese, and every other person who had been close to me had turned their back on me. That may not have been completely true, but it certainly felt like it. I thought that I had been dropped in the deepest ocean, far from any land, and had to swim to shore. I had no idea where to begin as I didn't know where to find the shore to put my feet on solid ground again. I began to wonder if there was something wrong with me. Was I sick? Was I evil? Why was my life such a disaster? Where was God when I needed Him most? Why had everything collapsed around me?

Needing help and in desperation, I went to a Christian counsellor, both for myself and for Elizabeth. It seemed there was nothing I could do to restore my life. At night, I went to bed in despair, and I greeted each morning in despair. I felt like a dead man walking through a barren wasteland. All I wanted to do was curl up and die. It did not take the counsellor long to discern that my past was affecting my present and would destroy my future, unless I was willing to deal with the ghosts in my closet. The ghosts in my life had been safely hiding in the basement of my soul for forty-one years. Did I have the courage to tell another human being what I had been through?

I confess I did not, as I didn't think anyone would believe the story of my past—and if they did believe me, what difference would it make? I had not told Doreen about my past, and certainly I never felt I could share it with Elizabeth. My counsellor, Dr. Becca Johnson, who has graciously endorsed this book, encouraged me to tell her my life story as far back as I could remember. She asked me to include every memory I could recall. But I found it hard to verbalize what had happened to me, so we agreed that I would write out my story as much as I could, and then we could start putting my life back together.

In a leap of faith, I did just that. It was twenty-five years ago that she helped me face what I had been through. After she read my story, she wrote to me and said, *"Ron, you were in fact actually, undeniably, unequivocally, horrendously, inexcusably, terribly, horrifyingly abused."* When I initially shared my story, I was amazed at how freeing it was to tell another person the truth about the first twenty years of my life. My biggest fear was telling someone the story and have them shame or dismiss me, because to me the story seemed too impossible for anyone to believe. Becca never shamed me, nor did she ever dismiss me. Instead, over the next two years, using my written story, Becca helped me rebuild my life. She began teaching me how to stop the never-ending tapes that constantly ran in my heart and mind that told me I was a failure and would never amount to anything. She helped me to realize that I was not a slave, a runt, or a piece of garbage. She helped me to see myself as a loveable person, so much so that Jesus hung on the cross and died for me. By this time in my life I had lost complete sight of God, in spite of my Damascus Road experience in 1979. I could see that Jesus would die for others and that God loved others, but I had an extremely hard time believing it for myself. I felt unlovable and saw myself as a complete failure as a husband and a pastor.

During my sessions with Becca, she would often write out Scripture verses that we had talked about, and I would post them on the walls of my study. It was not long before my study was wallpapered with these posters. Each passage was like a healing balm to my soul. Eventually these words moved from the posters to my mind and into my heart, where they became real. Becca helped me to see that I was a person who could be loved and who could love others. I was not an evil man, condemned to live in constant emotional pain for the rest of my life.

It was not enough just to be able to tell my story; I had another major step to take. With Becca's help, I also began the slow but exhausting process of forgiving those who had wounded me. Although I started this forgiveness work with Becca, I did not complete it until years later. Over time I had to learn how to forgive my father, my mother, my siblings, my schoolteachers, our family priest, and the sexual predator who had invaded my life. I also had to forgive Alice for the role she played in our lives in arranging our marriage. As step one of this process of healing and forgiveness, I decided that I needed to reclaim my family name, and so I legally changed my name back to Corcoran. Not only was it the right thing to do; when I had done this I felt I had reclaimed part of myself that I had so foolishly given away, and I felt whole again. It certainly raised eyebrows in the Diocese, but only the Reverend Harry Robinson wrote me a letter of understanding. I told the Diocese that I was in the process of being reconciled with my family, and as part of that reconciliation I wanted to reclaim my family name. With Becca's assistance I was able to reach out to my family, and over time I was successfully reconciled with each of them. Although I was never fully reconciled with my mother, eventually I was able to forgive her, and I will share more about that near the end of this book.

During this crisis in my life and marriage, the pressure in the parish continued to mount. Finally, when one more thing went wrong, I realized that no matter what I did, I would never win. My music director for the 9:00 a.m. worship service told me that she would be leaving. I had previously lost the rector's warden, the people's warden, the treasurer, and many members of the parish council. (For those of you who are not Anglican: these are the major leadership positions in an Anglican church.) The music director's announcement was the straw that broke the camel's back, and I decided it was time for me to leave the parish. In June 1993, I told the new church wardens of my decision and that I would leave the parish on the day the new building was scheduled to open—February 24, 1994. I had nothing left to give.

So I began the process of looking for a new parish, knowing that I might never find one that would want me. I applied to every diocese in Canada, except the Diocese of British Columbia, which was located on Vancouver Island. I had come to hate the west coast of Canada and could not wait to leave. Every application I sent out was rejected. Either nothing was available or I was not considered suitable. A friend in Birmingham, England, where I did the exchange, advised me that their rector had stepped down and they would be interested in having me as rector. This looked to be a win-win situation, as my friend was the chair of the selection committee. I had been there on an exchange two years earlier and I would have been willing to relocate in order to have gainful employment. In my heart I really did not want to go, but it seemed I would have to as there was nothing else. When the time came and the Diocese of Birmingham appointed a local candidate, I breathed a huge sigh of relief.

On the day I received that news, I lay down on my living room floor and said to God, "I give up! I don't know what you want with me, and I don't know where to go, and I hate my life. But today, I surrender to you once again. Take my life and do with it as you see fit. Amen!" The prayer took all of two minutes, and I got up from the floor and carried on with the rest of my day. I had once again surrendered to God and now my life was in His hands. That very evening, November 4, 1993, I received a phone call from St. Matthias Anglican Church in Victoria on Vancouver Island. They told me that they had heard about me from the Diocese of Montreal and that they would like to interview me for the position of rector of their parish. This was one of those God moments, and I knew immediately after I hung up the phone that I was going to Victoria. It was not that I *might* go to Victoria—no, I *was* going to Victoria, and I knew in my soul it was God's will. At the very last hour, God had opened a new door for me. I no longer hated the West Coast, but I would be absolutely delighted to leave Vancouver. I came to Victoria for the interview, and the following week I was told that I had been selected to be their rector.

I was looking forward to Victoria for a number of reasons, but there were two things I was hoping for more than anything else: First, I was looking for a fresh start as a pastor. There was no question I had to leave Vancouver, and I know that the parish was as anxious for me to go as I was. Second, I was hoping that after Ottawa, the Eastern Townships, Montreal and Vancouver God would also redeem our marriage. I thought a geographical change would make a difference. Although neither of us wanted to stay married, we still lived with the absolute belief that one day God would bless our marriage, because God told us to marry each other.

But Elizabeth did not want to move to Victoria. She wanted to go to Birmingham, as she firmly believed that she was in love with a friend of mine who lived there. She also believed that God was going to put them together. I did not know that she was fantasizing about this, but then I realized why she had put so much pressure on me to move to Birmingham and why she was so distraught when it did not happen. My friend in England was very happily married and he had absolutely no desire to enter into a relationship with Elizabeth. Unfortunately, falling in love with other men was a pattern in Elizabeth's life and part of the sickness from which she suffered. Eventually, my friend in England had to ask Elizabeth not to call or write any more letters.

Not long after we came to Victoria, our marriage fell apart completely. Our marriage had not at one time been ideal and then suddenly began to disintegrate. It had started as a lie, and after fourteen years of tremendous heartbreaking struggle, after seeing counsellor after counsellor, therapist after therapist and doctor after doctor, it was unravelling completely. During the year Elizabeth was in Victoria, she would phone me at the office every second or third day, threatening to harm herself. I would have to leave meetings, pastoral care sessions, or my everyday work at the office in order to respond to her. After a while I realized her calls were cries for attention. I did manage to get her to see a very competent doctor, who put Elizabeth on a new medication, but by that time, it was obvious to both of us and to others that there was something seriously wrong in our marriage. On our first Sunday at St. Matthias, we were going to be introduced to the congregation by the leadership. Elizabeth was not there. She was late for our very first Sunday service, even though we lived in the house next to the church. I knew at that moment that our marriage was ending and Elizabeth would not be staying in Victoria.

We had been in Victoria for a year when I met a local pastor who continues to play a role in my life. I told him about the state of our marriage, and he told me of an organization called *Wholeness Through Christ.* He thought this ministry would be able to help Elizabeth and me. Regrettably, by this time Elizabeth was living in a complete fantasy world. People would come to the rectory and knock on the door, but she would not answer, even though they could see her through the sheer curtains. She loved music and spent most of the day dancing behind closed doors. Anyone who came to the door was a distraction, which made her anxious. One Sunday, Elizabeth would come to church beautifully dressed and looking like a mature woman, and another Sunday she would be dressed in a totally inappropriate manner, like a teenager or even a child. She would often come into church and sit in the pew and cry, and tell anyone who would listen what a terrible person she was. Her behaviour by now was completely out of control and I had no more resources at my disposal. Her behaviour certainly affected my role and work as pastor. I was at my wit's end. When the priest who had told me of the Wholeness through Christ retreats mentioned that two counsellors were coming from England to lead a *Wholeness Through Christ* weekend, I asked if he could set up an appointment for Elizabeth and me to see them. I tried to get Elizabeth to come with me, but she refused, and so I went on my own.

I shared the sad story of our marriage with these two counsellors, and when I finished, I said to them, "My greatest difficulty with this marriage is that God told me to marry Elizabeth. But after fourteen years of marriage, I see absolutely no proof or any fruit of God's blessing on our marriage." Although many other things in my own life had changed, I had held on to that promise as a man clings to a lifeboat in the middle of a raging sea. That alleged word from the Lord was the only thing that gave me any sort of hope for our marriage.

When I had finished my story, one of the counsellors said to me, "Ron, I was a parish priest for over thirty years. I became a parish priest because my father was a bishop, and he told me that God wanted me to be a priest. I did not want to become a parish priest. I hated being a priest, and the moment my father died, I left the priesthood. Ron, I think you have been badly deceived, and that you and Elizabeth have been living a lie for fourteen years. From everything you have told me, I do not believe that this was ever a marriage." These words resonated in my heart, and I knew in an instant they were true. I drove home in a stupor; I was in absolute shock. I had allowed people complete power over my life, and as a result had lived and believed a lie for fourteen very turbulent years.

I went home and told Elizabeth that God had *not* told us to get married, and that we had been lied to. Elizabeth was as desperate as I was to find a solution and agreed to go and see this couple herself the next evening. I do not know what she told them, but she came home agreeing that we had been living a lie for fourteen years. It was not true that God said we were to marry each other. We faced the reality that we had finally heard the truth, and no matter the cost we needed the courage to set each other free.

That night I woke at 3:00 a.m. to find my pillow soaked with tears. I went into my study, lay on the floor, and cried my heart out to God. I felt that my heart was cracking in two. I had never been in such pain. I wept for all the wasted years for both of us, for all the dreams that were shattered, and for all our sorrow and disappointment. I did not leave Elizabeth because she was ill, and she didn't leave me because she didn't love me. No, right from the very beginning we were unevenly yoked and should never have married each another. We lost fourteen years because we gave someone else power and authority over our lives. What a price to pay because a small group of people thought they had the right to exert such weighty influence over us! As I cried, Elizabeth heard my sobs and came into the study. She said, "We could always stay together." But I replied, "No, we can no longer live this lie." A couple of weeks later, Elizabeth returned to the Eastern Townships outside Montreal, then back to Vancouver, and finally to London, Ontario, where she settled.

After she left, I had a dream that I remember in fine detail. I dreamed that on the day we got married, we left the church, and the next thing we knew, we were in a dungeon chained to opposite walls. Our chains could reach only half-way across the dungeon. We desperately tried to reach out or to touch each other, but each time the chains would snap us back against the walls. When I woke the next morning, the words of the song "Amazing Love" were reverberating in my heart. One of the verses says this:

Long my imprisoned spirit lay
Fast bound in sin and nature's night;
Thine eye diffused a quickening ray,
I woke, the dungeon flamed with light;
My chains fell off, my heart was free,
I rose, went forth, and followed Thee.
Amazing love! How can it be
That Thou, my God, shouldst die for me?[19]

I firmly believe that it was God who set us free. For fourteen years we had held up as an icon of belief, *"God wants you to get married,"* which in time became an idol that we clung to, especially in times of great difficulty. During all that time I waited for God to put His stamp of approval on our marriage. If our marriage was not something He had orchestrated, and if it was not His plan for our lives, how could He ever have blessed it? It was not possible. At every church wedding the familiar words *What God has joined together, let no man put asunder* are spoken. But what if God has not put it together? What happens when someone else puts it together in the name of God? What happens if someone deceives or manipulates you in a relationship that was never God's intention? What happens is that God gets blamed for all the failures of that relationship. I had made God my scapegoat. I had made Him totally responsible for the choices others had placed on me. I made Him totally responsible for the choices I had made because I was desperate to be loved and to be someone. Furthermore, I was frantic for Alice's approval and God's endorsement, as I believed that I was being obedient to the word of the Lord, as delivered to me by Alice and her prayer partner.

As things started to finally emerge from the darkness into the Light, I began to realize that I had been asking God to do

19 Charles Wesley, May 21, 1738

something impossible. I know now that God does not manipulate or coerce His children. I can say with confidence that the marriage between Elizabeth and me was not God's will for our lives. What grief and tragedy occurs in peoples' lives when others usurp the role of God! Such destruction is wrought in lives when individuals choose fleshly divination to control the lives of others. I accept full and total responsibility for my marriage to Elizabeth. Even though we were both coerced, we were still the ones who walked down the aisle and made the marriage vows. We were the ones who bore the consequences of our actions. I do not blame the group in Ottawa, or Alice, or Elizabeth. I am responsible for the choices I made.

It may seem in this narrative that I have been extremely hard on Elizabeth, but she did try her very best under circumstances that were totally beyond her control. She tried very hard to be a pastor's wife and to stand shoulder to shoulder with me, and there were times when she was more successful than others. Years later, Dr. Johnson told me that she thought that I was always honourable in my dealings with Elizabeth. No, I don't blame Elizabeth one iota for all the things that went wrong. I put the blame where it belongs. I blame the awful, hideous disease that she had to live with, day in and day out. Rejected at birth by her mother, her father was in prison, and her grandmother raised her to be a fearful person. The paranoid episodes in her life began in her teenage years, which resulted in hospitalization for long periods of time. Sometimes I wonder if it would have been helpful to have known each other's history prior to getting married. But when I think back to the bondage we were in while under Alice's control, I don't know if it would have made any difference. Would we have made different choices? Only God knows for sure! But I would never want anyone else to go through the torment and heartache that we experienced when we surrendered our wills to another to use us and control us for their own selfish reasons.

I recently read a devotional by Oswald Chambers, who said,

> One of the hardest lessons to learn comes from our stubborn refusal to refrain from interfering in other people's lives. It takes a long time to realize the danger of being an amateur providence; that is, interfering with God's plans for others . . . if there is stagnation in your spiritual life . . . you will possibly find it is because you have been interfering in the life of another—proposing things you had no right to propose, or advising when you had no right to advise.[20]

How different our lives would have been if others had heeded that counsel.

The minister who married us remained my very good friend, and after our marriage ended I wrote to him and told him that the relationship was over. Many years later, he confessed that he had not wanted to perform this wedding, and that he and his wife had been praying for us for years as he thought it inevitable that our marriage would fail. He described the marriage from its inception as *stillborn* and did not place blame on either of us when it ended in failure. He admitted that he also was intimidated by Alice and was caught up in her manipulation. He also told me that two other couples in the group who were married with Alice's help came to him for counselling, but because of pastoral confidentiality he was restricted in what he could tell me about their situations. But he did tell me that both couples

---

20 *My Utmost For His Highest,* Oswald Chambers, Dodd, Mead & Co., Inc. 1935 (republished 1992)

were being driven apart. Eventually one of the husbands ended up being institutionalized after a mental breakdown.

A couple of years later I travelled back to Ottawa to visit family members, and I decided while I was there I would take the risk and arrange a lunch with Alice. My motive for doing so was to try and find the answers as to why she went to so much trouble to have the two of us get married. At our lunch meeting she confessed that she thought Elizabeth's and my relationship would never last, but she flatly refused to take any responsibility for the mess she had created in our lives or the lives of others. I think in some ways I was looking for Alice to ask forgiveness for the destruction she wrought in our lives, but she didn't. It took me some time to find the grace to extend forgiveness to her and her prayer partner. Years later, out of the blue, she called me to give me her new address in case I ever wanted to be in touch. Needless to say, I will never travel down that road again.

After our marriage dissolved, I continued to care for Elizabeth financially, and I constantly remembered her in my prayers. Over time, as a result of her illness, Elizabeth reverted back to where she had been fourteen years earlier, receiving a disability allowance and under the care of social workers. I prayed that God would grant her peace, and I asked Him to impart wisdom to those who cared for her. In July of 2013, the Department of Social Ministries in London, Ontario returned my remaining support cheques for that year with a two-sentence letter saying that Elizabeth had passed away in May. I grieved for her as I recalled all the suffering she endured throughout her short life of fifty-seven years. But now she is in that place where there are no more tears, no more sorrows, no more grief and shattered dreams. Now she is totally free of the disease of paranoid schizophrenia. She is now the whole person God intended her to be. All I can say is, *Thank You, God! She has finally been delivered!*

Part III

DELIVERANCE AND REDEMPTION

March 1, 1994 – Present

"I will repay you for the years
The locusts have eaten,
The great locust and the young locust,
The other locusts and the locust swarm,
My great army I sent among you.
You will have plenty to eat,
Until you are full,
And you will praise the name of
The Lord your God,
Who has worked wonders for you;
Never again will my people be shamed…
There will be deliverance,
As the Lord has said,
Even among the survivors
Whom the Lord calls."
(Joel 2:25–27 & 32c)

CHAPTER THIRTEEN
A New Beginning

"'For I know the plans I have for you,' declares the Lord, 'plans to prosper you and not to harm you, plans to give you hope and a future. Then you will call upon me and come and pray to me, and I will listen to you. You will seek me and find me when you seek me with all your heart. I will be found by you,' declares the Lord." (Jeremiah 29: 11–13)

In 1994 my life changed once again. In March I began a new ministry at St. Matthias Church in Victoria, British Columbia, but during this time of transition I felt that I had run from the city of Vancouver with my tail between my legs as a complete and total failure. I was the pastor who had been invited to come, as I had been told, to save 'hedonistic' Vancouver five years earlier, but I had not saved anything. By the grace of God I had survived my time in Vancouver by the skin of my teeth. The problems began the day I arrived, and you now know the rest of that story. Although He may not have called me, I do believe that God used my time in Vancouver to refine me. On reflection, I confess I was arrogant, headstrong and filled with pride. However, I believe that God used the fires of my time at Holy Trinity to shape and mould me into the priest and pastor He wanted me to be—although when I left Vancouver, I was in a pretty shaky state. But then God used the congregation and friends in Victoria to love me from brokenness into wholeness. I can now look back and thank God for the learning that I went through in Vancouver, but I do not want to go back and settle there. Victoria is now my home and I am delighted to live here.

I remember my first service at Holy Trinity in Vancouver in 1989, when I preached on a text from Paul's letter to the church he pastored in hedonistic Corinth. In his letter, Paul said that during his ministry he was resolved "to know nothing while I was with you except Jesus Christ and Him crucified."[21] I confess that in my arrogance that is also what I wanted, and that is what I preached. But I didn't know what I was asking. To be crucified means to be willing to suffer and to die to self. Who wants to suffer? Who wants to die? I certainly didn't! I wanted the glory of saving Vancouver, but I certainly did not want to suffer or die in order to see that come to pass. Yes, in Vancouver I suffered, and unfortunately I didn't handle it very well.

So when I came to Victoria, I had absolutely nothing to lose. If I fell flat on my face in ministry for a second time, it would be the end of my profession as an ordained minister. I told God that if I failed this time, I would go to the nearest fast-food restaurant and apply for a job washing dishes in the kitchen and stay there for the rest of my life. I thank God daily that I didn't fail in Victoria. By God's grace it was a great success. I believe my ministry in Victoria was also a fulfillment of Paul's letter to

21 1 Corinthian 2:2

the Church in Corinth. Amazingly, it is the very next verse to the one I quoted above: "I came to you in weakness and fear and with much trembling."[22] Yes, I was weak and fearful, and my legs were trembling that very first Sunday I climbed into the pulpit.

Right from the very beginning in Victoria, the one thing that I felt I did right was to focus entirely on Jesus in my preaching and pastoral care. I concentrated on making my ministry in Victoria all about Jesus. When you honour and lift up the name of Jesus, what does He do in response? He does exactly as He promised: "I will draw all people to Myself."[23] That is exactly what He did, and I am eternally grateful. He gave me another chance. He sent me to a church that was hungry for God and to a people who wanted to make a difference in the world around them. I was honoured to witness numerous people give their lives to Christ and see long-time church members begin to realize their full potential as disciples of Christ. These disciples took care of each other in terms of sharing their goods, their homes and their gifts. Each year in the parish was better than the previous year. Most members of the congregation joined Bible study groups, supported overseas missions, and helped out in the city missions and were very active in the life of the diocese. On the pastoral side, people knit prayer shawls for the shut-ins, and my superb pastoral care team visited homes and hospitals on a regular basis. During my tenure as rector, I had leadership teams that were outstanding in terms of servant ministries. I quickly learned to trust them, and when they said they would take on a project, they carried it through to completion with enthusiasm.

After the majority of parishioners left St. Matthias Anglican Church of Canada, they became Christ the King and joined the Anglican Network in Canada in 2009. You can read the whole

22 1 Corinthian 2:3

23 John 12:32

story of that change in my book, *The Bishop or The King.* As Christ the King, we began a new ministry called *Living Edge* in the poorest part of Victoria. This ministry has thrived, and every Sunday now provides a hot meal for approximately 120-150 people. Two days a week it provides groceries for approximately 220 needy families. The majority of this work and its leadership came from the congregation that I had the joy of pastoring for twenty-one years. I can't begin to tell you how proud I am of these disciples taking on this project. In doing so they are fulfilling the mandate given by the prophet Isaiah: "You are to loose the chains of injustice and untie the cords of the yoke, to set the oppressed free and to break every yoke. You are to share your food with the hungry and to provide the poor wanderer with shelter; when you see the naked, to clothe them . . ."[24] As their former pastor, I salute them wholeheartedly as they carry out this Gospel mandate. If I am bursting with pride for them, imagine how God applauds them for their tremendous efforts on behalf of His Kingdom.

The staff I had during my twenty-one years at St. Matthias was extremely competent. I could freely assign tasks to the leadership and the staff and then step back and watch these leaders carry them out. There seemed to be no end to the many servant hearts that I inherited in St. Matthias. When I wrote my first book, *Jesus Remember Me*, I dedicated it to the praying saints and servants of St. Matthias. It was the highest compliment that I could render to them for their love and service to one another and their acceptance of me as their pastor. I loved them dearly, and they in turn dearly loved me.

When I first came to Victoria, I still carried a lot of grief and sorrow in my heart, even though I felt God's call. I had spent the previous two years digging through the basement of my soul

24 Isaiah 58:6–7

and I felt raw and extremely vulnerable. I also confess that my confidence as a preacher, pastor, and priest responsible for the souls of others was at an all-time low. In addition, my marriage was barely on life support, and I did not dare let anyone know how bad it really was, although I had to face the fact that the congregation would soon find out. I knew that I was still suffering some depression, and Elizabeth and I still felt trapped in our marriage and saw no way out of our predicament.

Having survived what I went through in Vancouver, I was desperate to make a success of things in Victoria, and I was delighted to have the opportunity for a new start. I know that during my first year in Victoria I was extremely insecure, and there were times when I felt like a diamond in the rough as I stepped on a number of toes! I had many rough edges that God had to smooth and I was also very aware that I needed to grow and trust the staff and the leadership team I inherited. Thankfully, in time that happened.

I was assisted tremendously in growing in trust from a very unexpected source. About eighteen months after I began my ministry in Victoria, the new rector and the rector's warden from my previous church in Vancouver came to Victoria to hand-deliver a letter to me. It was from the parish leadership of Holy Trinity in Vancouver. In the letter they apologized profusely for putting me in such an awkward position during my tenure with them and for all the pain and suffering I endured while trying my best to shepherd that flock. Part of the letter reads:

> *We know that we must repent, express contrition and forgiveness as individuals and as a community. Therefore, Ron, on behalf of the parish, we extend this expression of sorrow and request for forgiveness to Elizabeth and you; this is because you too*

> *have been hurt and harmed through our fault and contrary to the Gospel. Thank you for meeting with us today and considering our words of remorse and responsibility for our hurtful words and actions while you were the Rector of Holy Trinity.*

It was a wonderful, gracious and warm letter that I cherish today as one of the treasures that God has used to heal my soul. Any resentment or bitterness that I carried against that congregation and some of its leaders and members disappeared completely when I received their apology. It helped to lighten the burden I was carrying, and in the months ahead people in Victoria told me that I was relaxing and becoming more confident as their pastor and shepherd.

As I shared in the previous chapter, my marriage was at its breaking point when we moved to Victoria. It ended a year after my arrival, and at that time I thought I would have to resign. But because of the graciousness of my bishop, the parish wardens, the parish council, and the desire of the congregation, I was asked to stay as their pastor. I have no words to describe the compassion, mercy, and tenderness of the congregation towards me after I announced that my marriage had failed. The only people who were privy to my arranged marriage were the wardens, and they never broke that confidence. As a whole, the congregation came together and opened their hearts and their homes to me. They made sure that I was never alone for Easter, Thanksgiving, or Christmas. They were extremely receptive to my preaching and pastoral ministry. In spite of my many failures and shortcomings, they stayed committed to me and to the parish. Consequently I grew as a person and pastor.

Over the twenty-one years I was their pastor, I conducted close to one hundred and fifty funerals or celebrations of life. I also had the privilege of baptizing their children and grandchildren—marrying their children or at times their grandchildren. In seminary, we were advised not to get too close and to avoid making close friends with the congregation. I don't understand how you can possibly shepherd a flock if you don't love and nurture them. As a true shepherd you can't keep your distance from those to whom you are called to minister. You are called to be there in good times and in bad. You celebrate the weddings and the baptisms with great joy, and you weep with them at the loss of loved ones. You are called to manifest Christ's love, and the only way you can really do that is if you are in genuine relationship with those you are serving. Twenty-one years later, I would have to say that not only do many of them remain my friends—I look upon them as the family given to me by God. There are some members that reflect the love that grandparents pour upon their grandchildren. There are members that I look up to as parental figures. I confess that I am immensely blessed as I have lots of moms and dads who have shown me parental love. I am also blessed by having numerous brothers and sisters who I can play or pray with. Every pastor should experience at least once in their ministry the joy of serving in a congregation that truly loves them. What a gift from the hand of God!

After my marriage had finally collapsed, I knew that I needed to return to counselling. This time God chose a woman named Kandy who knew Becca from Vancouver. (I am privileged to have Kandy write the foreword to this book.) Kandy also worked out of a Baptist church. God had used Becca to help heal my childhood hurts and destroy the negativity that ran rampant in my life. Her counselling skills brought a lot of peace and comfort to my soul. She affirmed me and helped me to realize that indeed I was lovable and I was a child of God. Kandy taught me about moving into forgiveness, forgiving others, and receiving forgiveness for myself. As I had failed at marriage twice, I carried a lot of guilt and shame in my soul. With Kandy's assistance, I learned four lessons that had to do with forgiveness. It took me about five years of steady counselling to work out the healing of those lessons. Now you may believe that anyone who has been to seminary and is ordained would know a lot about forgiveness. That is true, and I knew that God was a forgiving God. I knew He would forgive others their sins—but would He forgive *my* sins? I had been told so many times that God could not possibly love me or forgive me and those falsehoods were buried in the basement of my soul. That was the tape that still from time to time reverberated in my mind. I truly did not know God's forgiveness for myself. Intellectually, I could grasp that truth, but I could not seem to move it eighteen inches from my head to my heart. Did God's forgiveness actually extend even to me? I knew God's forgiveness in the little things, but I did not know if He could or would forgive me my sins of failure in ministry and marriage. Was it possible for those specific sins to be forgiven and forgotten? Again the walls of my study were soon papered with posters of the reminders of God's faithfulness to forgive even the foulest sinners. For you who are reading this book, God has forgiven me and He will also forgive what you may consider the greatest failure in your life. (You will find in the Appendix a list of what others have said about forgiveness and some of what God has said about forgiveness in the Old and New Testaments. I memorized many of these in my healing process.)

The second thing I had to do with Kandy was to learn how to completely forgive my father and my mother for my lost childhood and adolescent years. After my encounter with God at my father's funeral, I found peace, and I believe that, on that day, I did forgive him and asked him to forgive me. I hope and pray that one day we will be reunited and we will be able to have a real and genuine relationship with each other.

I knew that I had a lot of work to do if I was ever going to get to the place where I could genuinely forgive my mother. The one time I attempted to talk to her about the abuse, she got up and walked out of the room. Then there was another time when she visited me once on the West Coast, and I was determined to take that opportunity to talk with her about my childhood. By this time she was in her mid-eighties and I did not want to blindside her, and so I was as compassionate and gracious as I could be. To this day I suspect my mother knew that I wanted to talk to her, but she did everything she could so that I would not have that opportunity. However, I knew it was now or never. So I took her to a restaurant, which I thought would be a neutral setting, so that she would be comfortable. But before I could begin the conversation, my mother began to speak. Out of the blue, she spoke to me for about forty-five minutes and told me about her childhood, which was also one filled with abuse. When she finished, I knew it would not have been appropriate at that moment for me to raise the subject of the abuse the three of us endured at her hands. I also did not know if what she told me was absolutely true or if she was manipulating me so that I would not talk to her about my own past. To this day I still do not know, but I decided to err on the side of graciousness and look for another opportunity to have a conversation sometime in the future. If what my mother told me was true, I thought that perhaps by revealing her own hidden past she wanted me to understand her abusive behaviour.

That day, I had to consciously let go of the things that I had wanted to share with her. I have since forgiven my mother, but the truth is we were not genuinely reconciled when she died at age ninety-three. My heart did not begin to heal until I was able to let go of the bitterness that had infiltrated my soul. There were other times when the two of us were together, but it never felt right for me to attempt to revisit this topic. My sister Annie, who witnessed the abuse, told me that Mother had shared with her that she regretted the things she did to us as children, and if she had the opportunity, she would say that she was sorry. The next time I went to Ottawa, I went to the nursing home where she lived, anticipating reconciliation. Although my mother knew why I had come to visit her, she was not able to deal with the topic. She skirted all around the issue but was not able to look me in the eye to say she was sorry. As she was then ninety-three, I realized that she did not have the resilience to disturb those ghosts. Regretfully, she died never having discussed the mistreatment of three of her thirteen children. To the best of my knowledge, she never discussed our upbringing with either Cynthia or Joseph. I have no doubt that the sins of the previous generation came down upon my generation, and I hope and pray that they did not carry on to the next.

I was in my mid-fifties before I was completely clear of the anger, hurt, and pain that had been stored in the very depths of my soul for so many years against my mother. Forgiving my mother took the longest time, but thank God, by His grace I was able to do so. My desire was to be completely reconciled with my mother and to hear her say just once, *I love you and I am proud of the person you have become.* I needed to let go of that expectation. However, God generously made provision for that dream to be realized and I will share that with you in the next chapter. It is very hard to describe the deep work in my heart that God has accomplished over the years around forgiveness for my parents. It is nothing less than a miracle of God's grace. I distinctly remember the day that I was able to say to God, *Please do not hold this sin against them*[25] and I honestly meant it! I confess that I did that because I want God to extend to me the same mercy that I was able to extend to my mother. I take seriously the words of Christ that the "standards we use to judge others are the same standards by which we will be judged."[26] If I want mercy for myself, then I must also grant mercy to others.

The third person that I also needed to forgive was Alice, for her spiritual manipulation of Elizabeth and me, which led to a marriage that was bound to fail from the very beginning. As I shared earlier, Alice Clarke remains a conundrum to me. When I met Elizabeth, Alice was very involved in Elizabeth's life. She may have seen me as a way of unburdening herself of the heavy load she had undertaken in nurturing and trying to love Elizabeth. I did not know how the Spirit of God worked, but I assumed that He worked through people like Alice. So when Alice spoke, it was as if God was speaking directly through her to me. As a result of this relationship with Alice, I learned a very important lesson: as a pastor, I have absolutely no right to direct the lives of others. I know first-hand the consequences of such actions. I give them my best advice, but the person who has come to see me is the one who has to make the final decision. Their decision may be life-changing, and they have to live with the consequences of their decision. I always invite people to come back to see me and have me pray with them after they have made their final decision. They are the ones who have to take ownership and bear the responsibility of what they have decided to do. As a consequence of the spiritual manipulation that took place in my life by letting others make decisions for me, I let resentment grow in my heart. How could I forgive myself for the anger and bitterness I had carried in my heart for years towards God? How could I forgive

25 Acts 7:60

26 Matthew 7:1-2

myself for allowing Elizabeth and me to get so caught up in the spiritual foolishness that had robbed us of a good portion of our lives? We were so unevenly matched; how could I forgive myself for the many conflicts that occurred in our marriage? It was as a result of spiritual foolishness that I never became a father, and will never be a grandfather. I cheated myself of those blessings.

The fourth thing that I had to work through with Kandy was sorting out what role did the Evil One play in my life? There is no doubt in my mind that some of what happened to me and my siblings was evil. What doors in my life did I open to allow him to wreak such havoc? I will talk about this briefly in the last chapter of this book.

Over the years, I learned the hard lesson of how to forgive others so that their sin would no longer influence my life. That meant not only forgiving my father, mother, and Alice—I also needed to forgive Bill and Doreen, my siblings, the sexual predator, school teachers, priests, and some of the members from the congregation in Vancouver. I also needed to know how to extend God's generous forgiveness to myself. As a result of being sinned against, I harboured envy, rage, hatred, selfish ambitions and jealousy in my heart. It was an American missionary who said, "In order for God to get the light in, the darkness has to be brought out."[27] The more I yearned for the light, the more the darkness fled. God means it when He says in the Lord's Prayer that He will forgive us our trespasses as we forgive those who trespass against us. The emphasis is on the word *as;* if we are not willing to forgive others *as we have been forgiven,* we tie God's hands in being able to extend to us His forgiveness. (See Appendix II for a general prayer of forgiveness for others.)

Dear readers, if I could leave you one truth about forgiveness and reconciliation, it would be this: Time *does not* heal all

27 Coco Mullins, *In the Tears of a Wounded Child*, Xulon Press, 2002

wounds—*forgiveness* heals wounds. However, we need to fully understand that forgiveness does not necessarily mean reconciliation with the person who wounded you. In some cases it is possible, but in others, it is not. However, reconciliation is not the goal of forgiveness. On the cross, Jesus said to those who ordered his death and crucifixion: "Father, forgive them, for they know not know what they are doing."[28] After His resurrection, Jesus did not sit down and break bread with the Roman soldiers, Pontius Pilate or Caiaphas. Those going through the painful process of forgiveness must remember to keep their expectations of restoration and reconciliation realistic. That takes time to learn, because at one point I thought forgiveness also meant reconciliation. Although I have fully forgiven my predator, I have absolutely no interest in being in a relationship with him. There are some people that you forgive while also keeping them at arm's length, (for example, Alice), as they are not safe people. I firmly believe that God understands that completely. It was His Son who said to us in the Sermon on the Mount, "Do not give to dogs what is sacred; do not throw your pearls to pigs. If you do, they may trample them under their feet, and turn and tear you to pieces."[29]

---

28 Luke 23:34

29 Matthew 7:6

CHAPTER FOURTEEN
The Divine Romance

"A wife of noble character—who can find? She is worth far more than rubies. Her husband has full confidence in her and lacks nothing of value. She brings him good, not harm, all the days of her life…many women do noble things, but you surpass them all. Charm is deceptive, and beauty is fleeting; but a woman who fears the Lord is to be praised. Honour her for all her hands have done and let her works bring her praise at the city gate." (Proverbs 31: 10 & 29-31)

When I came to St. Matthias in March of 1994, I was given new life. I had previously been introduced to the parish council, and now I was introduced to the staff. One of those staff members was Deirdre McCann. It took me about six weeks to finally pronounce her name correctly. Deirdre was the most competent administrative assistant anyone could ever have. Daily she arrived at work early and often left late. She was an extremely conscientious worker. She knew all the members of the congregation, and which ones needed pastoral care and the ones who needed to be ministered to with gentleness or a firm hand. Deirdre was also what I would describe as a righteous person. She had standards that she was not willing to compromise and she was an absolute joy to work with. She was extremely discerning and knew shortly after I arrived that my marriage was suffering. Because of the many phone calls I received from home I would return to the office stressed or very preoccupied. She never crossed boundaries by asking me awkward or embarrassing questions, but remained steadfast and supportive as she observed our marriage coming off life support. She was more than gracious to Elizabeth and did everything in her power to establish a good rapport with her. Years later she told me that although Elizabeth was congenial, her strange behaviour and inappropriate comments were red flags to Deirdre. Again, years later, Deirdre found out why I left the office so often to go back to the rectory as I was very worried that Elizabeth would take her own life.

When my marriage ended, I thought that I would lose Deirdre as my assistant as the divorce of her pastor and boss caused her a great deal of pain. Years later, Deidre had to fill out forms for the diocese, and she wrote:

> I actually wondered if I could continue to work with Ron as I was intolerant of divorce. I have always believed that any relationship could be salvaged through prayer and counselling. However, I realized that I was judging Ron for making the choice to end his marriage and it was not my place to do so. In hindsight, I realize that there are some relationships that cannot be

> reconciled. I had never experienced divorce from this perspective before, and having witnessed the pain and suffering that Ron went through, and how he agonized over providing for Elizabeth, I am now at peace with their situation.

She also wrote that she came to a new understanding of divorce:

> Furthermore, through research, study, and prayer, I now have a more compassionate heart and a deeper understanding for those involved in divorce. I know as it says in Scripture that the Lord hates divorce; however, I believe we serve a loving and compassionate God who extends His grace to those who have failed. Could I do any less?

Although I was Deirdre's supervisor for five years before she left St. Matthias to take up another position as the administrative assistant in a school, we developed a tremendous relationship of friendship and mutual respect for one another. And while our relationship was always professional, it changed one Christmas around an innocent conversation about Christmas decorating. About mid-December, I asked Deirdre if she had her Christmas tree and house decorated. She replied, "No," as it had been two years since she last decorated for Christmas. Deirdre and her father used to decorate the tree together and she could not bring herself to do so since her father had passed away. She was very close to her dad and could not imagine decorating for Christmas without him. I spontaneously volunteered to come and assist her to set up the tree. Although Deirdre was single, her mother lived with her, and so the three of us would be involved in this

Christmas activity. I was aware that it would not be appropriate for me to be alone with Deirdre, but with her mother present I felt it was perfectly suitable.

When we began to unpack the lights for the tree, Deirdre discovered numerous notes written to her by her father. The notes explained that the lights had been checked, and also reminded Deirdre which lights were to be hung where. It was a great surprise to Deirdre that her father had written these notes, and it turned out to be a very emotional evening for Deirdre and her mother. They shed many tears over these notes and the fact that her father was not here with them to celebrate the season that he loved so much. That was the start of a beautiful friendship.

From time to time Deirdre's mother would invite me to dinner, not in any attempt to match-make, but she could see that we had formed a very deep friendship with each other. I think the most important thing about our relationship was the tremendous respect we had for each other. As the years went on, other parishioners would host dinner parties, and from time to time they would include the two of us as their guests. Again, I don't think that people were attempting to put us together, but they could see that we had a very special God-fearing, respectful relationship.

This was put to the test when a parishioner came to me and wanted to interview Deirdre for a position at a Montessori school. I was extremely reluctant to give permission as I thoroughly enjoyed working with Deirdre and did not want to lose that relationship. So I didn't say anything for a season about this request to Deirdre, but over time I felt it would be inappropriate for me to withhold the possibility of this employment opportunity from her. Due to all her skills and graces, the school didn't hesitate to hire her, and subsequently I lost her as my assistant.

There is an old expression that has been credited to a Portuguese bishop: *God draws straight through crooked lines.* When Deirdre left my employ, I thought that would be the end of a very special relationship built on trust and mutual respect. Again, years later, when Deirdre had to fill out forms for the diocese, she wrote about her time at St. Matthias and working with me:

> During the time I have worked with Ron I have seen him at his best and his worst. Through it all, he has been a man of integrity and compassion. I genuinely like him as a person . . . I respect and admire Ron; he has a true pastor's heart and is always willing to go the extra mile. I know his history and I commend him for the way in which he has dealt with his failures and heartache. Ron has always treated me with respect . . .

When Deirdre began working at the school, the person who was supposed to train her left the very day that Deirdre started, and this caused Deirdre tremendous stress. So periodically her mother would call and invite me to dinner to talk and pray with the two of them. I am absolutely positive that Rose did not have any ulterior motives, but our relationship continued to grow deeper and deeper. Over time, I realized that I wanted to spend the rest of my life in Deirdre's company—not once in a while, but all the time. But in order to be fair to Deirdre, I had to tell her the whole story of my past. I knew that I could never enter into a full and blessed relationship without telling Deirdre the complete truth about my upbringing and my failed marriages. It took some time to share with her all that you have read in Part I and Part II of this book. But I was bound and determined not to enter into an intimate relationship with another person unless they knew my entire history. I had no idea at that time if Deirdre would consider pursuing a personal relationship with me, but I took the risk and told her my story. She was only the third person to whom I had revealed the deep and inward parts of my soul. Deirdre's response was one of compassion, mercy, and empathy. There was no judgment of my marriage failures, nor did she ever convey anything but understanding and love as I shared my background.

In the fall of 1999, I asked Deirdre if she would be willing to be my wife; Deirdre's immediate response was, "I don't know. I need time to think about this." She had not been married and was content being single. So within the next few days, Deirdre wrote out 150 questions that she wanted to ask me about marriage and what our life would look like if we did get married. It took some time to answer them, but it also gave me a chance to ask my own questions so that we would not end up in a conflict-driven marriage. The advantage Deirdre had in marrying a pastor is that she had first-hand knowledge of the pros and cons of full-time pastoral ministry. After we finished answering each other's questions, we thought it would be wise to see a marriage counsellor and ask the counsellor to take us through a Marriage Enrichment program. The counsellor told us afterward that we attained a perfect score when it came to communication, which we both believe is the most important component in a great marriage. So it was now time to ask the question, and I did so on April 23rd, 2000, which happened to be Easter Sunday. By the way, she responded with a resounding *'YES.'* But before I asked for her hand in marriage, I knew that I had to do three things:

First, I had to go to my Heavenly Father and ask His blessing for this marriage. I was not willing to take any sort of risk without feeling extremely confident in my soul that this was God's plan for our lives. As I had failed at marriage, I wanted

God's permission and blessing to marry Deirdre, and I believe I received it. Sixteen years later the abundant fruit of our marriage is obvious for all to see.

Second, out of respect for Deirdre's mom, I went to ask her blessing, as our marriage would certainly turn Rose's life upside down. She and Deirdre had lived together since the death of her husband, John, eight years earlier. Rose generously gave her blessing.

The third thing that I had to do, out of respect for the fourth commandment of honouring my mother and father, was to call my mother and request her blessing. That I could even make that call showed me how much I had grown and matured in forgiveness. My mother didn't quite understand what I was asking. At first, she thought I was asking for her permission. I assured her that I did not need her permission, but out of respect for the fourth commandment I wanted her blessing. In the end my mother gave it to me.

The following Sunday I announced to the congregation that I was going to make a life change and that I had asked Deirdre to marry me. The response from the congregation was overwhelming. I can't remember how many people came up to us and told us, "We have been praying for this for years."

Deirdre and I thought it would be about a year by the time we had things organized and we would be ready to marry. However, as I said in the last chapter, I had an outstanding congregation, which was further confirmed to me as they organized the wedding—all we had to do was show up. What a gift from the church family! All we had to do was put together the service; the congregation decorated the church and organized the reception. Two of our parishioners gave us a gift of a wedding supper at an elite hotel here in Victoria, and one of our parishioners arranged for the honeymoon suite at another hotel. We were richly blessed from beginning to end.

One of my closest friends was my best man, and my other best friend performed the ceremony. That day at church there were 364 people in attendance, and it was one of the highlights of the calendar year. It was a typical Irish wedding, with a full choir and three clergy to make sure we were well and truly married. The only complaint we heard from others was that the wedding service, which lasted for over two hours, was too short! Some said that they did not want it to end.

We discovered two months after the wedding that my dear friend from New Brunswick, who married us, did not have a licence to perform the wedding in British Columbia. In the eyes of God we were certainly married, but in the eyes of the province, they were not so sure. We all had a great laugh over the licence omission. All we had to do, however, was sign affidavits to prove we were really married—after all, we did have 364 witnesses.

Deirdre and I agreed that it would be unfair to ask her mother to live alone after she had been living with Deirdre for eight years. So eventually we found a house with a beautiful suite for Rose. As I wanted this marriage to be utterly successful, I suggested we sign a covenant agreement and establish some boundaries. I wanted to be sure that Rose would not interfere with our marriage, and at the same time we would not interfere with her life. I thought I was being very clever and careful. I suggested in the covenant that Rose could join us for dinner once a week. On the first night after we returned from our honeymoon, I asked Deirdre what Rose was doing for supper. Deirdre said she was probably preparing her own supper and eating it by herself. I couldn't stand that. I had eaten alone for far too many years and I know how lonely having a meal on your own can be.

So I called and invited Rose up to join us, and that was the end of the covenant as she ate with us every night from then on. Not once in the seven years we lived with Rose did she ever interfere with our relationship. She was so respectful of our boundaries and was a tremendous blessing to both of us. Regretfully, Rose ended up with Alzheimer's disease, and for her own safety we had to place her in a care home, where she died in 2009.

Part of the parental healing that I received came through my gracious mother-in-law. She became the loving, affectionate mother that I never had. Rose was the one who again and again affirmed me as a man and as her son-in-law. She was proud of me and often told me. When I came home from work at night, I would go and visit Rose in her suite, and she welcomed me with a smile, a kiss, and all the news. I would sit on the couch in her living room and put my arm around her shoulder as she told me about her day. Unfortunately, I was never free enough to be that demonstrative with my own mother. God used Rose to continue the process of healing my heart and my memories. When I sat with her and shared my day, she would stop what she was doing and pray with me. When my feeling memories or wicked dreams would surface, she was the one who put her arms around me and knew the exact prayer to pray. She was an extremely gracious woman, and her compassion and love for me was the healing balm that I needed on my journey to wholeness. Rose has been gone for six years now and I miss her every single day. I miss her presence, her love, support, compassion and prayers. She would often say to me, "You are the son that I never had who loves the Lord," and I would often respond, "You are the mother I never had who loves the Lord." Rose was one of the most generous gifts that God saw fit to pour into my life, and I can't wait until the day I see her again. Although there are many women who have redeemed motherhood for me, it is fair to say that God used Rose more than any other woman to heal the deep wounds in my soul.

Though I never met Deirdre's father, from her description of their relationship I almost feel as though I know him. Others who knew him in Victoria have described him as a wonderful godly man and they would all be delighted to have him as a father. When we married, Deirdre gave me his Celtic cross, which I have worn faithfully ever since. I guess I have some of the same characteristics and habits as Deirdre's father, for she often says to me, "As long as you are alive, my father will never be dead." Deirdre tells me that she has no doubt that John and I one day will have a great and awesome relationship for eternity. Again, I can't wait!

Our marriage has been sixteen years of absolute bliss. Many have commented on our marriage, saying that we are a gracious example of a blessed union. We believe that we model for others what marriage should be. The diocese in which I served for fifteen years has also always been very complimentary of the fact that Deirdre and I were no longer working together when our relationship turned from friendship to love. They have held up our marriage as an example for other clergy couples.

I will always remember a clergy retreat that I attended, where the main speaker met with each of us for healing and prayer. We were asked to review our lives and to share our greatest disappointments. I shared about my broken marriages, and the speaker said to me, "I want you to go back to your room and read the story about Jesus turning water into wine in John, chapter two." He added, "Ron, God always saves the best wine until the end."[30] He certainly did!

That word has come to pass. From the moment we married we have been content and richly blessed. The day I walked down

30 John 2:1–12

the aisle to the back of the church and took Deirdre's hand in mine and walked up the aisle to the altar, there was absolutely no doubt in my mind and heart that Deirdre was exactly the woman that I chose to marry. We are indeed each other's best friend. Every day, we pray together and share openly our dreams and desires. There isn't a night we go to bed without cuddling and thanking God for the gift He has given to us in each other. Deirdre is always a joy to wake up next to, always cheerful and full of life and genuine Irish laughter. Rarely a day goes by when she doesn't make me roar with laughter with something she does or says. I readily confess that Deirdre has spoiled me, and God has used her to restore for me my birthday, Christmas, Easter and Thanksgiving, and all the days in between. As we both were a little older when we got married, I asked the Lord for at least twenty-five years together. But now that sixteen years have passed so quickly, I am asking for an extension of another twenty-five years. If the Lord tarries, that is what I want!

In our sixteen years of marriage, we have had only one difficulty worth mentioning: When Deirdre was working, she left earlier in the morning than I did. Prior to leaving she would bring Rose her breakfast on a tray, and she would also bring me breakfast in bed. What a treat! However, the first couple of times she brought me breakfast, I responded in fear. I was sleeping, and once again I could hear my mother's footsteps coming down the hall to get me out of bed, and it would bring me back to my childhood. After I responded in fear a number of times, I realized the impact this was having on Deirdre. It broke my heart to see the pain I was causing her by unconsciously reacting the way I did. We went to see Kandy and she prayed us through the memories; after that, I never again awakened in fear and trembling when Deirdre brought me breakfast in bed.

From time to time I have horrendous nightmares when something triggers my haunting memories from the past. As I was writing this memoir, there were nights when I would wake up screaming, but Deirdre was always there to comfort and pray for me until I was able to fall back to sleep. I know without a doubt that I am a very blessed man who has indeed found a "noble wife." The day that Deirdre and I were married, we danced to one song, and the words of that song have remained part of our life. It would be selfish to keep those words to myself, and so I will share them with you with the hope that one day you also will find that indeed *'There is a Place'* where dreams come true. It happened for me; it can certainly happen for you.

Deep down inside
Inside my soul I feel passion and fire
I've got a yearning that words cannot express
A hunger for love and tenderness

Deep down inside
I know you feel the hunger and so do I
When the wonder of a fairy tale will never fail

There must be a place
Where dreams come true
There must be a time
When I'm free to fly
There must be a place

Deep down inside
Inside my heart I'm falling
One more time
Overtaken by the promise of love
That I have been made a captive of

Deep down inside
I'd do anything if only I could find
Find all the memories of once upon a time
I wanna to make them mine

There must be something inside of me
That keeps believing in love
What is this something inside of me
That knows there's so much more
Make it all worth living for.[31]

Yes, the Lord has restored the years the locusts have eaten. But why did the locusts steal those years?

31 (*"There Must Be a Place"* from the album *Father's House*, by Brian Doerksen. Used by permission.)

CHAPTER FIFTEEN
Why, Why, Why

"Peace I leave with you; my peace I give you. I do not give to you as the world gives. Do not let your hearts be troubled and do not be afraid…In this world, you will have trouble. But take heart! I have overcome the world." (John 14:27 & 16:33)

As I read through my old prayer journals, I found these words, from an unknown author: *Until I told my story, I could forgive them, but I could not love them.* I can honestly say that I have finally learned to love those who caused me so much heartache. Love for those who hurt me is in my heart, not because I am such a wonderful person, but because God is a gracious and loving God. He healed my heart of the pain, sorrow, and disappointment I have endured on my journey through life. My primary desire when I began this writing was to share some of my trials and experiences so that it might bring light and healing to others who have had to endure similar difficult paths. My prayer is that my story will help those who need to be healed, to be able to forgive those who wounded them so severely, and to embrace forgiveness for themselves.

But anyone reading this book may ask the same question that I asked. WHY? Why did these things happen? One of the great dangers of the *why* question is that you can get lost in the unquenchable desire to know the answers. When you can't find the answers, you may find yourself lost in bitterness and anger, which is exactly where I found myself. I know from experience that constantly thinking about or even becoming addicted to finding the answers of "why" can lead to spiritual, mental, and emotional torment. You may never find the answer to the question. Maybe *why* is not the right question.

A very wise man once shared with me that *why* is not as important as people think. The question should really be twofold: First, what can God do with the suffering a person endures? And second, what can God do with the mess?

As I said earlier, I believe that the greatest gift God has given us is the gift of free choice or free will to use as we see fit. Some in my life deliberately chose to use their gift to manipulate, torture, abuse, and satisfy their own lusts and desires. Life is always about the choices we make. As a consequence of what I suffered at the hands of my abusers, I made some very poor choices, and that is why I can honestly say that I made a mess of my life. Others may have contributed to that process, but at the end of the day, I bear the responsibility for the choices I made. For example, I have complete free will to seek healing from the wounds I endured, or I also have the free will to live in the past and dwell in the pain that I suffered. Again, I also have the free choice to forgive others or to hold bitterness and resentment against them. God will not force me to extend forgiveness to others, but I will have to suffer the consequence of that free choice. The question for all of us is;

which *wolf* will I feed? Here is a little illustration of what I am talking about.

> "One evening an old Cherokee told his grandson about a battle that goes on inside people. He said, "My son, the battle is between two wolves. One is Evil. It is anger, envy, sorrow, regret, greed, arrogance, self-pity, guilt, resentment, inferiority, lies, false pride, superiority and ego. The other is good. It is joy, peace, love, hope, serenity, humility, kindness, benevolence, empathy, generosity, truth, compassion and faith." The grandson thought about it for a minute and then asked his grandfather, "Which wolf wins?" The old Cherokee simply replied, "The one you feed."[32]

If we choose not to forgive, it is likely that our life will be shaped by bitterness and anger. In fact, we can become addicted to bitterness and anger. We may feel that we have every right in the world to hold onto our wounds—and of course we can. However, there is no question that carrying those burdens will lead to spiritual, mental, and at times physical death. Why? Basically because we are being eaten alive from the inside out; the poison within us is destroying our soul.

Let me share with you a true story of a former parishioner named Maggie who has now gone to glory. Maggie was a member of my parish in Vancouver, and she and I developed one of those mother and son relationships. When I came to the parish, I had been warned by many people never to cross Maggie. Most had given up on her and described her as a bitter, angry old woman, and if you crossed her, there was no doubt the

32 http://www.oneyoufeed.net/tale-of-two-wolves/

sparks would fly. So I was advised to steer clear of her if I was going to survive in this parish.

Several weeks after my arrival, I went to have tea with Maggie. During our time together, she told me that when she was a little girl she broke her wrist. A doctor had reset it, but he had been intoxicated while performing the surgery, and when the cast was removed, the wrist had been set wrongly. For the rest of her life, her right hand was for the most part useless. When she returned to school, the other children teased and taunted her about her misshapen wrist and hand. Consequently, she had suffered great sadness during her childhood, with more than her share of shame and embarrassment.

As Maggie got older her situation didn't improve much. Because of her handicap, her employment was tenuous and she never married, so I understood how the bitterness in her soul had taken root. During our visit over tea that afternoon, she shared her disappointments in life, and in her history in the parish (where she had been a member for over sixty-eight years). I asked her what would happen to her when the Lord came to take her home. Her immediate response was that she would go to purgatory to pay for her sins and maybe one day she might get into heaven.

I spent the rest of the afternoon telling her the Good News of Jesus Christ, reminding her that Jesus Christ came into the world to save all sinners. He didn't punish His children by sending them to purgatory to pay for their sins—He had already paid for them in full. Maggie was genuinely shocked by the Good News that I shared. Before I left her that afternoon, she bowed her head, and for the first time in her life invited Jesus into her heart and forgave the doctor who caused so much heartache in her life.

The following Sunday I had three services, one at 8, one at 9 and the 11:15, which Maggie attended. When I came to robe for that service, members of that congregation and some from the 9:00 a.m. service wanted to know what had changed Maggie. Overnight, Maggie was transformed. Her face was bright, her spirit was light, and there was joy in her voice. She was a brand new person. The bitterness, anger, and disappointment had been swallowed up in Christ. This wasn't a temporary change; this was a lifetime change, and her transformation caught everyone's attention. Even though people talked about the Good News and God's ability to change lives, they didn't really believe that God was capable of reaching Maggie—they thought the outside shell was too hard and the inward spirit beyond repair.

Maggie was in her early eighties when she came to Christ, and in her late eighties she finally went home totally at peace with God. She became one of my dearest friends, and to this day, I sorely miss her. I was a first-hand witness to what God did for Maggie, and I desperately wanted Him to do that for me. And that is exactly what He did. My transformation did not take place overnight, but nevertheless it did take place.

It is only fitting to finish this memoir by sharing with you three characters from the Bible and how each of them helped me understand my own suffering. All three of them suffered unjustly, but they stand today as true conquerors over unjust suffering. I am not going to quote a lot of Scripture, but I invite you to take a Bible and read the passages that I mention when you finish reading this book.

The first conqueror is my dear friend *Job*. The Book of Job is one of the most profound and one of my favourite books of the Bible. According to some theologians, this book may be older even than the book of Genesis; some have suggested that Job lived during the time of Abraham, and the book may have been written during that time. The rest of the Scripture writers certainly thought Job was a real person as he is mentioned in both the Old and the New Testaments. The Book of Job is based on Job's concern about his faith in a Sovereign God. Can this Sovereign God be trusted? Is He good and is He just? Job seems to ask, *Why do good people suffer undeservedly?* Suffering troubles all of us, but most of all we do not understand undeserved suffering, and, rightfully so, we seek viable explanations for that suffering.

Over the years, Job has become my friend, and I read him when I am burdened by the troubles of life. I read him when I am in despair, in physical pain, in mental anguish, and when I feel like a social outcast. I read him when I feel I am going through the valley of the shadow of death and the dark night of the soul. I read him when I need reminding that God is just and good. Admittedly, God is not always understandable, but He is always just and good along with being sovereign and all-powerful.

In the first two chapters of his story, Job is stripped of everything.[33] Who stripped him of his family, possessions, and health? It was not God. No, but with God's permission, it was the Evil One. Today there is no doubt in my heart or mind that the Evil One wreaked havoc in my childhood home. There is no question that he played a role in Bill and Doreen's unfaithfulness and that he orchestrated my marriage to Elizabeth. He certainly was a factor in the divisions that took place in Vancouver. In each of the above circumstances, he gained a foothold in our lives through the sin that took place in the dark behind closed doors. One of Jesus' closest friends who succumbed to temptation and sin later wrote, "Be alert and of sober mind. Your enemy the devil prowls around like a roaring lion looking for someone to devour. Resist him, standing firm in the faith, because you know

33 Job, Chapter 1–2

that the family of believers throughout the world is undergoing the same kind of suffering."[34] There is an enemy in our world who hates God's creation and God's children, but we make a grievous error if we blame everything that happens in our lives on him. It was the moralist CS Lewis who wrote:

> "There are two equal and opposite errors into which our race can fall about the devils. One is to disbelieve in their existence. The other is to believe, and to feel an excessive and unhealthy interest, in them. They themselves are equally pleased by both errors, and hail a materialist or magician with the same delight."[35]

Some people dismiss the Evil One as an impersonal force or somebody in a red suit with a pitchfork. On the other hand, there are many who attribute too much power and importance to him. They feel he is God's equal. In the story of Job, and in Jesus' teaching, we see that the Evil One is restrained by God in his power to do harm. He is not omnipotent but as Peter says, he is always seeking someone to devour.

The Apostle Paul also cautions us not to give the devil a foothold, because when we do, he takes over and wreaks havoc in the lives of God's children. I failed and I opened the door for him to gain a foothold in my life, but with Jesus I have an Advocate. What does my Advocate do? He prays for all of us. In his Epistle to the Romans, Paul wrote: "Jesus is on the right hand of the Father, and is interceding for us."[36] Not only do I have a heavenly intercessor, now I also have numerous saints in countries all

---

34 1 Peter 5:8

35 CS Lewis, *The Screwtape Letters,* (Macmillan Paperbacks Edition, 23rd Edition 1976)

36 Romans 8:34

around the world who are more than willing to intercede for me. When I was a child I thought I was so alone, but now I know that I had a prayer warrior who for decades specifically prayed for me and for my brother, Joseph.

As I told you in Chapter Two, my grandmother had a great influence on the lives of Joseph and me. Grandmother once spent two weeks with my sister Cynthia, my brother Joseph, and me. At the end of her visit, she called Joseph and me into her bedroom and asked, "What do you want to be when you grow up?"

Joseph responded immediately: "I want to be a priest."

His answer upset me as I thought it was the perfect response. We recognized our grandmother as a holy woman of God, and after two weeks of joy and celebration we wanted to please her with the right answer. So I answered and said, "I also want to be a priest."

In 1987, I was ordained a pastor in the Anglican Church, and in 1988 my brother Joseph was ordained a minister in another denomination. Between us, we have spent sixty years in pulpits sharing the Good News of the Gospel of Christ. I imagine my grandmother thought we would become Roman Catholic priests, but we both believe God had other plans for our lives.

After I was ordained, I travelled to Prince Edward Island, and out of love and respect for her, I visited her graveside. Although I knew she was in heaven, I went there to say, *Thank you for all your prayers; I am here to tell you they have been answered.*

Let us return to my friend Job: For thirty-five chapters in the book, Job tries to convince his friends that he is not a sinner, and his friends try to convince him that he is in fact a secret sinner, and that God is punishing him by stripping him of his family, possessions, and health. Job wants to haul God into court and place Him in the witness box; he is convinced that he will find

God guilty and therefore will win his case against Him. He is persuaded that he is above reproach and should not be punished for anything, as Job believes he is totally righteous and God is at fault. By the end of chapter thirty-seven, Job and his friends have entered a stalemate; they literally have run out of words. In the previous chapters, Job demanded no less than thirty-six times that God speak to him.[37] Finally Job and his friends fall silent, and that is when God speaks.

It is in chapters thirty-eight to forty-one that God speaks to Job out of a storm. For 129 verses God reminds Job that He alone is Creator God and He does not need Job's help in running the universe. He has been doing it for centuries and will continue doing it for eternity. God describes His awesome activity in creating and sustaining the world and wonders if Job can match His work. At the end of His speech, God finishes by asking Job if he is in a position to judge Him. God points out that it is extremely impertinent of Job to even think that God should explain Himself. Interestingly, in those four chapters God never once gives Job an explanation for his suffering.

The novelist and Presbyterian theologian Carl Frederick Buechner wrote:

> "Maybe the reason God doesn't explain to Job why terrible things happen is that He knows what Job needs isn't an explanation. Suppose that God did explain . . .And then what? Understanding in terms of the divine economy why his children had to die, Job would still have to face their empty chairs at breakfast every morning. Carrying in his pocket straight from the horse's mouth a complete theological

---

37 Job Chapters 3–36

> justification for his boils, he would still have to scratch and burn."[38]

What difference does it make if we understand all the reasons for evil, sin and suffering? Theological explanations cannot heal the soul, only God can do that. It is when you share your story with therapists and skilled counsellors that you begin the process of healing of the soul. So what does Job do in response to God's chastisement? He did the only thing possible: he repents.

> "I know that you can do all things; no purpose of yours can be thwarted. You asked, 'Who is this that obscures my plans without knowledge?' Surely I spoke of things I did not understand, things too wonderful for me to know. You said, 'Listen now, and I will speak; I will question you, and you shall answer me.' My ears had heard of you, but now my eyes have seen you. Therefore I despise myself and repent in dust and ashes."[39]

At one time I was very much like Job. I wanted to know why I suffered the way I did. What was the purpose of my suffering? Why was I confronted with so much evil in my youth? Why was my childhood stolen from me? And as this book relates, there are many other whys. I have concluded that the *why* is not as important as it once seemed. I no longer need vengeance for my life to be fulfilled. I need love, mercy, tenderness, and forgiveness, and those are things that I receive freely from God. If I freely receive those things from God, how can I even think of withholding

---

38 Carl Frederick Buechner, *Wishful Thinking, A Theological ABC*, page 47 (New York: Harper and Row, Publishers, 1973)

39 Job 42:1–6

them from others who have sinned against me? I do not have that right.

I recently finished reading Laura Hillenbrand's book, *Unbroken*. It is a true World War Two story of survival, resilience, and redemption, and it was on the New York Times bestseller list for three years. The main character, Louis Zamperini, is dealing with the aftermath of being constantly and brutally beaten and dehumanized in a Japanese prisoner of war camp. One of the guards stripped him of his dignity and left him feeling humiliated, ashamed, and powerless. Louis believed that the only way for him to be free was for this guard to suffer and to die in the grip of Louis' hands. Once the war was over, Louis believed that for freedom to manifest in his life, it would be necessary for him murder the guard. The author writes this very poignant truth: "The paradox of vengefulness is that it makes men dependent upon those who have harmed them, believing that their release from pain will only come when they make their tormentors suffer."[40]

Like Louis, I believed that I needed to exercise vengeance on those who abused me. With God's healing power in my life, the time came when all I could do was cry out, like Job, in repentance to my Heavenly Father. Remember, as I confessed earlier in this book, at one time, I was the man who wanted to force the crown of thorns down upon the head of Christ. I was the man who badly wanted to drive the nails into Christ's hands and feet. I was the man who wanted to pick up a cat of nine tails and whip Christ. I was the man who wanted to put his hands around Christ's neck and squeeze the life out of Him. Who did I think I was? I shudder with the memory of how much anger I stored in

40 Laura Hillenbrand, *Unbroken*, page 373 (Random House Trade Paperback Edition, 2014)

my soul towards God. I can only do what Job did: repent. This was my prayer:

> Father, forgive me for my distorted thinking and the rage I carried in my heart. Lord Jesus, thank you for absorbing my sins in your body on the Cross. Holy Spirit, once again I thank you for opening my eyes to see.

Some regard the grace and forgiveness of God as their absolute right. Those of us who have done things that we are deeply ashamed of marvel at the amazing grace and amazing forgiveness of the Father. Those who accept this grace know that they don't deserve it, and they can only accept it with grace and gratitude. Those who sincerely appreciate and understand forgiveness are those who have truly needed it.

The second conqueror I want to draw to your attention is my Biblical friend *Joseph*. The story of Joseph and his brothers is told in the book of Genesis from chapters 36–50. That must tell you how important this story is, as there are fourteen chapters based on these brothers. I am not going to review all fourteen chapters, but I will give you a synopsis of the story. We know from reading those chapters that Joseph was not very well liked by his siblings. He was a bit of a tattletale[41] and a dreamer, and Jacob, his father, made no secret of the fact that out of his twelve sons, Joseph was his favourite. Imagine how the other eleven brothers felt about this. But their father compounded the dissension in the family by providing Joseph with an ornate robe, which down through the ages has been known as the *coat of many colours*.[42]

One day the father sent Joseph out into the desert to see how his brothers were managing the sheep. But instead of going

---

41 Genesis 37:2

42 Genesis 37:3

incognito and keeping a low profile, Joseph went out wearing his flashy coat. From a distance the brothers saw Joseph coming and they plotted to kill him. When he arrived, they stripped him of his coat and threw him in a cistern to die. They planned to soak the coat in animal blood and bring the coat back to the father and tell him that a ferocious beast devoured Joseph. One of his older brothers did not want to kill him. He thought he could rescue him and send him back to his father alive. But when this older brother left to do some errands, a caravan passed by and they changed their plan. They decided instead of killing him they would sell him and at least get something for his life. So they sold him for a pittance and the leaders of the caravan took Joseph to Egypt. The text doesn't tell us how old Joseph was when this happened, but he must have been in his early teens. When his brothers returned to their father with his colourful coat, the father broke down and declared that he would spend the rest of his life mourning Joseph.

Meanwhile, Joseph was sold to the pharaoh of Egypt, and over time Joseph became the right-hand man of the pharaoh. But Pharaoh's wife had her eye on Joseph, and when he refused her advances, in retaliation, she decided to accuse Joseph of molesting her. I am not sure that the pharaoh actually believed her, because he imprisoned Joseph instead of having him put to death. We don't know how long he was in jail, but he was released when he was able to interpret Pharaoh's dreams of a famine that was going to strike Egypt for seven years. There were to be seven years of prosperity followed by seven years of famine.

Joseph was placed in charge of the country, second only to Pharaoh. The Scripture tells us that Joseph was thirty years old when he was appointed to this position. So from the time he was sold until he was released from prison, approximately seventeen years had passed. During the seven years of prosperity, Joseph stored up grain in order to help Egypt survive the seven years of famine that were to come. But the famine didn't only affect Egypt—it also affected Canaan where Joseph's family lived. Joseph was probably in his forties when his brothers came from Canaan to Egypt to buy grain. If they sold him as a teenager, it is not hard to understand why they did not recognize him when they encountered him in Egypt.

It was Jacob who sent Joseph's brothers down to Egypt to buy the badly needed grain, but in order to buy grain, the brothers had to meet with Joseph. Only ten of the brothers went to Egypt as the youngest, Benjamin, stayed home with his father. When the brothers came into Joseph's presence he immediately recognized them, but none of them recognized him. Joseph didn't let on that he knew them. But by questioning the brothers, he found out that Jacob was still alive and that his brother Benjamin had remained behind with his father. Joseph sold them the grain, but insisted if they wanted to return to buy more grain, they must bring their youngest brother Benjamin with them to prove they were not spies. More time passed, and the brothers came back to buy the badly needed grain, but Joseph, through twists and turns, threatened to arrest Benjamin and make him a slave. But his brothers pleaded with Joseph, saying that if Benjamin didn't go back with them, their father would die of a broken heart. It was at that moment that Joseph broke down and revealed to them that he was their brother whom they had sold to the Egyptians out of jealousy approximately twenty-five or thirty years earlier.

I tell you this whole story so that you will know Joseph's attitude toward his brothers. He was not bitter or resentful. In fact, he said to his brothers, "And now, do not be distressed, and do not be angry with yourselves for selling me here, because it was to save lives that God sent me ahead of you."[43] During those years of separation, Joseph grew into a man of God—so much so that he could see the purpose of his suffering.

In time, his father and the rest of his family moved to Egypt, and the nation of Israel was saved by Joseph, the one who was sold into slavery. When Jacob died, his brothers once again lied to Joseph and said that their father told Joseph to forgive the brothers for their actions. When Joseph heard their request, he broke down and he said to his brothers, "Don't be afraid. Am I in the place of God? You intended to harm me, but God intended it for good to accomplish what is now being done, the saving of many lives."[44]

Looking back on my life, those words resonate with me: *what others meant for evil, God meant for good.* I wonder if I had not experienced the tribulations I went through, would I have given my life to Christ? Would I have become a man entrusted by God to faithfully proclaim the Gospel of Jesus Christ to others? Would I have become the man who fell in love with God and still burns today with a passion to tell others about Christ? I honestly don't know. Did I have to go through all I did to bring me to Christ? No, I don't believe I did, but those tragedies did bring me to the foot of the Cross, and thirty-seven years later I can honestly say, what others meant for evil, God meant for good. I absolutely love what Paul wrote in his Epistle to the Romans:

> "And we know that in all things God works for the good of those who love him, who have been called according to His purpose. For those God foreknew He also predestined to be conformed

---

43 Genesis 45:5

44 Genesis 50:19

> to the image of His Son, that He might be the firstborn among many brothers and sisters. And those He predestined, He also called; those He called, He also justified; those He justified, He also glorified."[45]

My third and final conquering hero I hold up to you is *Jesus Christ, the Son of the Living God.* As I sit in my study and write these lines, we are entering into the Christmas season. So many in our world do not understand the primary reason why Jesus came into our world on that first Christmas just over 2000 years ago. He didn't come to give us a temporary glow in our heart during this festive season. Jesus Christ came to earth for the express purpose of dying for our sins and removing the sting of death. He died for me and He died for you. He certainly didn't die a normal death; He died on a cross, crucified between two thieves. He came as the perfect sacrifice for the sins of this whole world. He came and took my sins and your sins, and my suffering and your suffering, upon Himself. When I compare my suffering with the suffering of Christ, I must admit I have barely suffered. If you want to truly appreciate all Jesus did for us in terms of suffering, all you have to do is read Psalm 22 and Isaiah 52:13 to 53:12. They describe in detail the suffering which Christ endured for all of us. The four Gospels do not detail Christ's sufferings as clearly as these passages. The Gospel writers focused their attention on Christ's short ministry of three years and His glorious resurrection, but they also include His suffering, death, and burial. The Christian God did not triumph over evil by destroying it, but by absorbing it. (He became sin for us.) He transformed victimization into resurrection, and it is in the

45 Romans 8:28-39

resurrection that we find hope and new life.[46] I would summarize the story of Jesus' death as found in the four Gospels in this way:

Jesus was betrayed for thirty pieces of silver by one of His closest friends. While at prayer, He was arrested in the Garden of Gethsemane. His disciples, who had walked with Him for three years, fled in terror. He was taken to the Sanhedrin where He was spat on, struck, and slapped. He was bound and taken to Pilate, who sent Him to Herod, where He was ridiculed, mocked, and then returned to Pilate. Pilate released the criminal Barabbas at the demand of the people, had Jesus whipped, after which the soldiers stripped Him, dressed Him in a scarlet robe, crowned Him with a crown of thorns, mocked Him, spat on Him, and struck Him. They put His own clothes back on Him, and made Him carry His cross to the place of execution. According to tradition, Jesus met His mother on the way to the Place of the Skull. With courage and grace, He said to her, "Mother, I am making all things new." At the Cross, spikes were driven into His hands and feet and He was scorned by the religious leaders, mocked by the soldiers, and sneered at by one of the criminals crucified with Him. When He died, a Roman solider drove a spear through His side into His heart, to make absolutely sure that He was dead.

Jesus endured it all without complaint or anger. Years later, His friend Peter the Apostle wrote,

> "When they hurled their insults at Him He did not retaliate; when He suffered, He made no threats. Instead He entrusted Himself to Him who judges justly. He Himself bore our sins in His body on the cross, so that we might die to

46 Joanne Feldmeth & Midge Finley, *We Weep for Ourselves and Our Children* (Harper, San Francisco, 1990)

> sin and live for righteousness; for by His wounds you have been healed. For you were like sheep going astray, but now you have returned to the Shepherd and Overseer of your souls."[47]

When I suffered and was offended, I did not entrust myself to God. Instead I wanted revenge, on the perpetrators as well as on God. I did not suffer in silence, and if I did I made sure that I stored the rage, bitterness and anger in my heart. In contrast, Jesus took all that His enemies did to Him without complaint. Where was God while Jesus suffered? Paul says, "God was in Christ reconciling the world to Himself."[48] As Jesus suffered, God suffered. While we are suffering, we often feel that we are alone, but God promised in His Word that we are never alone. Although we may not see Him or sense His presence, He is always there.

The 1986 Nobel Peace Prize holder, Elie Wiesel (mentioned earlier in the prologue) shared this story, which I included in my book, *Jesus Remember Me*. As a teenager, Elie was taken to the Auschwitz and Buchenwald concentration camps, and he recorded his experiences in his book, *Night*. He witnessed evil at its most shocking and absolute, and records being forced to watch the cruel hanging of a young boy:

> For more than half an hour he stayed there, struggling between life and death, dying in slow agony under our eyes. And we had to look him full in the face. He was still alive when I passed in front of him. His tongue was still red; his eyes were not yet glazed. Behind me, I heard a man asking, 'Where is God now?' And I heard a voice

---

47 1 Peter 2:23-25

48 2 Corinthians 5:19

> within me answer him: *Where is He? Here He is—He is hanging here on this gallows . . .*[49]

Jesus knows what it is like to hang on the gallows, for He hung on a cross for our sake. At times we ask, "Where is God when evil, sin, and injustice run rampant in our world?" In spite of all that takes place in this world, evil will not have the final word. If you are searching for God in the midst of tragedy and terror, you will find God present in those events. Sometimes it is extremely hard to see Him or sense His presence, but He is there. God is present in the school halls where the innocent have been slain. God walks the streets of our cities, embracing the homeless and the hungry and those experiencing devastating pain. God is present in the homes of those whose lives have been torn apart by abuse or neglect, and in homes where chaos reigns. God is not a stranger to those who have been terribly abused, nor is He a stranger in refugee or concentration camps. He is there weeping with those who weep, and granting courage to those who are in despair.

A final truth I would like to share with you in this chapter comes from a man I consider a friend. I have met him only once, but his books have been my companion and helper on my road to wholeness. His name is Philip Yancey. In his book, *Disappointment with God,* he taught me a simple truth. He wrote:

> Life is unfair—God is fair. We all need to stop confusing God with life. Was life fair to Jesus? The cross demolished forever the basic assumption that life is fair. The cross of Christ overcame sin and evil, but it did not overcome unfairness.[50]

---

49 Wiesel, Elie , *Night,* tr. Stella Rodway (New York: Bantam Books, 1958, 1982) 62

50 Yancey, Philip, *Disappointment with God, (*New York: Harper Paperbacks, 1991)

CHAPTER SIXTEEN
Deliver Us From Evil

Jesus said: "This, then, is how you should pray: Our Father in heaven, hallowed be your name, your kingdom come, your will be done, on earth as it is in heaven. Give us today our daily bread. And forgive us the wrong we have done, as we have forgiven those who have wronged us. And lead us not into temptation, but *deliver us from the evil one." (*Matthew 6:9-13-NEB/NIV)

I began writing this book in September, 2014 at Ste. Anne de Kent in New Brunswick. My friends have an apartment they rent on the Northumberland Strait. It is a wonderful restful setting to do this work. By the time this book is published it will be almost twenty-four months of continual writing and re-writing. My editors have gone through eleven drafts of the book. This will give you an idea of how difficult it was to write and how patient my editors have been.

As I wrote there were two issues with which I wrestled. First, would I dare publish this work and second, how would I title the book. In the Introduction and Prologue I shared my reasons for writing the book. I wrote to encourage others so that they may find their own deliverance and redemption. I wrote for those who have been severely wounded and are going through life feeling unloved and unwanted. God loves you and regardless of what you have been through, you have tremendous value in His sight. Many people have been physically, mentally, spiritually, sexually or verbally abused. They live with the scars and the wounds that have never been healed. My story shows that all those wounds can be healed and the years that you have lost can be redeemed. One of my concerns while writing was that some may see this memoir or others like it as a form of exhibitionism; I believe that those who risk telling their stories do so, for the most part, in the hope of helping others. That is my desire.

A recent article in the Telegraph[51] in London, England tells the story of Archbishop Justin Welby, the Archbishop of Canterbury, head of the worldwide Anglican Communion. He discovered through DNA testing that the man he thought was his father for over sixty years was actually not his biological father. His biological father, the former secretary to Winston Churchill, had a liaison with the Archbishop's mother just prior to her marriage. His parents were addicted to alcohol and Justin Welby said: "As a result of my parents' addictions my early life was messy…" (He and I have that in common.) Archbishop Welby goes on to say: "My own experience is typical of many people. To find one's father other than imagined is not unusual. To be the child of families with great difficulties in relationships with substance abuse or other matters is far too normal…even more importantly, my role as Archbishop makes me constantly aware

51 *The Telegraph News,* April 26, 2016

of the real and genuine pain and suffering of many around the world…although there are elements of sadness and even tragedy in my father's case, this is a story of redemption and hope from a place of tumultuous difficulty and near despair in several lives." General opinion is that the Archbishop has handled this news with grace, and since he has the courage to let others know the secrets buried for over 60 years, I do the same. We have found our identity in Christ and the desire to spend our lives sharing Christ with others and helping them find hope. If what I have encountered in my life will bring transformation to others, then telling my story has been worthwhile.

My second struggle was to find an appropriate title. I started with the title, *Deliver Us From Evil.* This changed to, *Fear No Evil.* I considered *Be Not Afraid.* Then the title was going to be *Redeemed* as this is a book about Redemption. Finally I returned to *Deliver Us From Evil* as this book is not only about Redemption, it is also about Deliverance. You cannot enjoy the fruit of Redemption if you have not experienced Deliverance. Deliverance is the cry of the heart. *Deliver Us From Evil* came from Jesus' words in the prayer He taught His disciples, generally known as *The Lord's Prayer.* It could be called The Prayer of Humanity. We need deliverance from evil. Isn't "Deliver Us From Evil" the unspoken prayer of the child who is being bullied or abused? Isn't it the prayer of the abused man or woman caught in loveless and hopeless situations? I am sure it is the prayer of those fleeing as refugees from war torn countries. Evil seeks to destroy and to cause havoc in peoples' lives and unchecked it carries on from one generation to another. Evil is very powerful and strong. However, it is my absolute belief that evil is not a match for Christ. Christ overcame evil, sin and death and He did so at the cross. God has declared that there is no other name under heaven which can bring complete deliverance and redemption.[52]

This book is not only about suffering but also about Deliverance and Redemption. I have walked for thirty-seven years in a day-by-day relationship with Christ. There were many times when I took my eyes off Him and slipped back into the pit of despair, but He prevailed. When I committed my life and my future to Him, He promised: "He who began a good work in you, will carry it on to completion until the day of Christ Jesus."[53] I know that what He started, He will finish, not only in my life, but also in yours.

I hope you have recognized that no matter how grievously you have been wounded by another, their sin is forgivable. God will give you the grace to do so. In his book, *Voyage to Alpha Centauri,* the Catholic writer, Michael O'Brien, explained it well. The father in the story cautioned his son, who had discovered that his siblings had been murdered. The son wanted justice and declared that he would hate the perpetrators all his life. His father said: "Do not hate them. They do not know they are evil. They are blind. If you hate them, if you kill them in your heart, they will not die. They will rise up again and again within you, and they will kill your heart."[54] I know from personal experience this is true, please don't let it happen to you.

Some readers might be tempted to judge and "throw stones" at those who abused a young boy so grievously. You might be tempted to criticize those who spiritually led him astray when all he wanted to do was follow God. Please don't "throw stones" or criticize. I have forgiven and have asked God *not* to hold those sins against my perpetrators. I could not do this in my own

52 Acts 4:12

53 Philippians 1:6

54 Michael O'Brien, *Voyage To Alpha Centauri*, pp 343

strength, but through the grace and mercy of the loving God who has also forgiven me. Luke's Gospel tells the story of Jesus' encounter with a sinful woman at the home of a Pharisee. The Pharisee objected to Jesus' lack of discernment in dealing with this 'so called' sinful woman. In reply Jesus says: "Her many sins have been forgiven-as her great love has shown. But whoever has been forgiven little loves little."[55] My many sins have been forgiven by a compassionate God and I cannot help but love Him, and in turn by His *grace* forgive those who severely wounded me.

If you are a person who has caused grievous harm to another, know that your sin is forgivable. May God give you the grace to repent and make restitution where possible and yes, he will show you how to do so. If you are angry and bitter at God, He understands and invites you to tell Him. I did, and to my astonishment I discovered that He is a loving, understanding, and compassionate God. If you are a person carrying regret, sorrow, and sin, I pray that God will meet you, as I know that is His chief desire.

I am compelled to tell you how passionately God loves you. You may not know it. What others have planned for evil, God will one day use for good. I am an example of what God can do when we turn to Him with all our heart. "'You will seek me and find me when you seek me with all your heart. I will be found by you,' declares the Lord."[56]

In closing, I would like to finish off this book with a blessing that I use when closing off services in the church: "Go forth into the world in peace; be of good courage; hold fast to that which is good; render to no person evil for evil; strengthen the faint hearted; support the weak; help the afflicted; honour all people; love and serve the Lord rejoicing in the power of the Holy Spirit.

55 Luke 7:36-47

56 Jeremiah 29:13-14

And may the blessing of God Almighty, the Father, the Son and the Holy Spirit be upon you and those you love this day and forever more. Amen."

Finally, once again I say:

Soli Deo Gloria:
To God alone be the glory

APPENDIX I

Below are the words I prayed on the 29th of May, 1979, when I invited Jesus into my life. I have carried this prayer in my wallet for the past thirty-six years:

> Lord Jesus Christ, forgive me for my sins. I open the door of my life and receive you as my Saviour and Lord. Take control of the throne of my life and make me the kind of person you want me to be.
>
> Thank you for coming into my life and for hearing my prayers as you promised. Thank you dear Jesus.

PRAYER OF FORGIVENESS

> Lord, I forgive [name those who hurt you]:
>
> Lord, please take any judgment or bitterness out of my life. I do not want these sins in my heart and I ask you to remove them. Please bring your healing balm to places of my life where I

have been wounded and please forgive me where I have sinned. I choose not to blame or hold sins against others. I also relinquish my right to be paid back for my any losses that I have suffered and I completely forgive the ones who have sinned against me. In saying this prayer I am declaring my trust in God, alone who is the Righteous Judge.

ABOUT FORGIVENESS

Below you will find what some of the giants of the faith have had to say about forgiveness, and what the Scriptures of the Old and New Testament proclaim. These sayings and passages were the ones that God used for healing in my life. May He do the same for you in your healing process.

Forgiveness is surrendering my right to hurt you for hurting me.[57]

We are most like beasts when we kill. We are most like men when we judge. We are most like God when we forgive.[58]

Forgiveness is God's invention for coming to terms with a world in which despite their best intentions, people are unfair to each other and hurt each other deeply.[59]

---

57 Archibald Hart, cited by James Dobson, *Love Must be Tough* (W Publisher Group, 1983)

58 William Arthur Ward, *Thoughts of a Christian Optimist* (Drake House, 1968)

59 Lewis B. Smedes, *Forgive & Forget, Healing the Hurts We Don't Deserve* (Harper One, 2007)

Forgiving is not forgetting. You can never forgive people for the things you have forgotten. You need to forgive precisely because you have not forgotten what someone did; your memory keeps the pain alive long after the hurt has stopped.[60]

Forgiveness is as indispensable to the life and health of the soul as food is for the body.[61]

OLD TESTAMENT

Because of the Lord's great love we are not consumed, for his compassions never fail. They are new every morning; great is your faithfulness. (Lamentations 3:22–23)

Can a mother forget the baby at her breast and have no compassion on the child she has borne? Though she may forget, I will not forget you! See, I have engraved you on the palms of my hands. (Isaiah 49:15–16)

As a father has compassion on his children, so the Lord has compassion on those who fear him; your walls are ever before me. (Psalm 103:13)

I will give you a new heart and put a new spirit in you; I will remove from you your heart of stone and give you a heart of flesh. (Ezekiel 36:26)

60 Lewis B. Smedes, *Forgive & Forget, Healing the Hurts We Don't Deserve* (Harper One, 2007)

61 Myron Augsburger, *The Communicator's Commentary — Matthew* (Word Publishing, 1987)

For as high as the heavens are above the earth, so great is his love for those who fear him; as far as the east is from the west, so far has he removed our transgressions from us." (Psalm 103:11–12)

And he passed in front of Moses, proclaiming, "The Lord, the Lord, the compassionate and gracious God, slow to anger, abounding in love and faithfulness, maintaining love to thousands, and forgiving wickedness, rebellion and sin. Yet he does not leave the guilty unpunished; he punishes the children and their children for the sin of the parents to the third and fourth generation. (Exodus 34:6–7)

If my people, who are called by my name, will humble themselves and pray and seek my face and turn from their wicked ways, then I will hear from heaven, and I will forgive their sin and will heal their land. (2 Chronicles 7:14)

"Come now, let us settle the matter," says the Lord. "Though your sins are like scarlet, they shall be as white as snow." (Isaiah 1:18)

NEW TESTAMENT

For all have sinned and fall short of the glory of God, and all are justified freely by his grace through the redemption that came by Christ Jesus. (Romans 3:23–24)

Blessed are those whose transgressions are forgiven, whose sins are covered. Blessed is the one whose sin the Lord will never count against them. (Romans 4:7–8)

But God demonstrates his own love for us in this: While we were still sinners, Christ died for us. (Romans 5:8)

The death he died, he died to sin once for all; but the life he lives, he lives to God. In the same way, count yourselves dead to sin but alive to God in Christ Jesus. (Romans 6:10–11)

For the wages of sin is death, but the gift of God is eternal life in Christ Jesus our Lord. (Romans 6:23)

Therefore, there is now no condemnation for those who are in Christ Jesus. (Romans 8:1)

You were washed, you were sanctified, you were justified in the name of the Lord Jesus Christ and by the Spirit of our God. (1 Corinthians 6:11)

Godly sorrow brings repentance that leads to salvation and leaves no regret, but worldly sorrow brings death. (2 Corinthians 7:10)

I have been crucified with Christ and I no longer live, but Christ lives in me. The life I now live in the body, I live by faith in the Son of God, who loved me and gave himself for me. (Galatians 2:20)

In him we have redemption through his blood, the forgiveness of sins, in accordance with the riches of God's grace. (Ephesians 1:7)

For He has rescued us from the dominion of darkness and brought us into the kingdom of the Son He loves, in whom we have redemption, the forgiveness of sins. (Colossians 1:14)

But when the kindness and love of God our Savior appeared, he saved us, not because of righteous things we had done, but because of his mercy. He saved us through the washing of rebirth and renewal by the Holy Spirit, whom he poured out on us generously through Jesus Christ our Savior, so that, having been justified by his grace, we might become heirs having the hope of eternal life." (Titus 3:4–7)

For if you forgive other people when they sin against you, your heavenly Father will also forgive you. (Matthew 6:14)

But I want you to know that the Son of Man has authority on earth to forgive sins. (Mark 2:10)

Do not judge and you will not be judged. Do not condemn, and you will not be condemned. Forgive, and you will be forgiven. (Luke 6:37)

And with that he breathed on them and said, "Receive the Holy Spirit. If you forgive anyone's sins, their sins are forgiven; if you do not forgive them, they are not forgiven. (John 20:22–23)

If we confess our sins, he is faithful and just and will forgive us our sins and purify us from all unrighteousness. (1 John 1:9)

BIBLIOGRAPHY

Writing on this topic has been difficult, but I have found the following extremely helpful in this writing. Although I have not quoted from all of these resources, they were so very helpful in my healing process, and may also be of benefit to you.

Allender, Dr. Dan and Longman III, Tremper, *Bold Love* (NavPress, 1992)

Allender, Dr. Dan, *The Wounded Heart* (NavPress, 1990)

Augsburger, Dr. Myron S., *The Communicator's Commentary, Volume 1* (NT) Matthew, (1987)

Bonhoeffer, Dietrich, *Discipleship Vol. 4* (Fortress Press, 1989)

Buechner, Carl Frederick, *Wishful Thinking: A Theological ABC* (Harper and Row Publishers, 1973)

Chambers, Oswald, *My Utmost for His Highest*, updated edition (Oswald Chambers Publications Association, Ltd, 1992)

Colson, Charles and Pearcey, Nancy, *The Problem With Evil* (Tyndale Publishing, 1999)

Colson, Charles, *Justice that Restores* (Tyndale House Publishers, 2001)

Colson, Charles, *Who Speaks for God?* (Crossway Books, 1985)

Corcoran, Ron, *Jesus Remember Me* (Clements Publishing, 2004)

Corcoran, Ron, *The Bishop or the King* (Essence Publishing, 2009)

Crabb, Larry, *66 Love Letters* (Thomas Nelson Publishers, 2009)

Dickens, Charles, *The Christmas Carol* (Chapman & Hall, 1843)

Felmeth, Joanne Ross and Finley, Midge Wallace, *We Weep for Ourselves and Our Children* (Harper Collins Publishers, 1990)

Frank, Jan, *Door of Hope* (Thomas Nelson Inc., 1993)

Frankl, Victor E., *Man's Search for Meaning* (Beacon Press, Boston, 2006 Edition)

Green, Peter, *Watchers by the Cross* (Longmans Green & Co., 1934)

Guinness, Os, *Unspeakable* (Harper Collins Publishers, 2005)

Hart, Archibald, *Love Must be Tough* (W. Publisher Group 1983)

Hillenbrand, Laura, *Unbroken* (Random House Trade Paperback Edition, 2014)

Hughes, Selwyn, *Every Day With Jesus* (CWR, Booklets 1993-2007)

Ingram, Chip & Johnson, Dr. Becca, *Overcoming Emotions That Destroy* (Baker Books, 2009)

Jacobs, Cindy, *Possessing the Gates of the Enemy* (Chosen Books, 1991)

Johnson, David and Van Vonderen, Jeff, *The Subtle Power of Spiritual Abuse* (Bethany House Publishers, 1991)

Johnson, Becca Cowan, *Good Guilt, Bad Guilt* (Intervarsity Press 1996)

Irene Kelly, *Sins of the Mother* (Pan Books, 2015)

Kennedy, Sheldon with Grainger, James, *Why I Didn't Say Anything* (Insomniac Press, 2006)

Kushner, Rabbi Harold, *When Bad Things Happen to Good People* (1st Anchor Books Edition, 2004)

Lewis, C. S., *Surprised by Joy* (Geoffrey Bles, 1955)

Lewis, C. S., *The Screwtape Letters* (MacMillan Publishing Co. Inc., 1959)

Lloyd Jones, Sally, *The Jesus Story Book Bible* (Copyright 2007)

Lloyd-Jones, D. Martyn, *Studies in the Sermon on the Mount* (Intervarsity Press, 1959-60)

Merriam-Webster, *Webster's Ninth New Collegiate Dictionary,* 1984

McDowell, Josh, *Undaunted* (Campus Crusade for Christ, 2012)

McGee, Vernon, *Through the Bible, Joshua to Psalms* (Nelson Publishers, 1982)

McMillian, Dr. S. I., *None of These Diseases* (Ravell 2003)

Mullins, Coco, *In the Tears of a Wounded Child* (Xulon Press, 2002)

O'Brien, Michael, *Voyage to Alpha Centauri* (Ignatius Press, 2013)

Pawson, David, *Unlocking the Bible* (Harper Collins Publishers, 2003)

Pelzer, Dave, *A Child Called "It"* (Omaha Press, 1993)

Pelzer, Dave, *The Lost Boy* (Health Communications, 1997)

Rivers, Francine, *Bridge to Haven* (Multnomah, 2014)

Smedes, Lewis B., *Forgive & Forget, Healing the Hurts We Don't Deserve* (Harper One, 2007)

Solzhenitsyn, Aleksandr, *The Gulag Archipelago* (Thomas Whitney, 1974)

Stott, John, *The Spirit, the Church and the World* (Intervarsity Press, 1990)

Ten Boom, Corrie, *The Hiding Place* (Chosen Books, 1971)

Ward, William Arthur, *Thoughts of a Christian Optimist* (Drake House, 1968)

Wiesel, Elie, *Night* (Hill and Wang, 1972)

Wright, N.T., *Evil and the Justice of God* (Intervarsity Press, 2006)

Yancey, Philip, *Disappointment with God* (New York: Harper Paperbacks, 1991)

Yancey, Philip, *Vanishing Grace* (Zondervan, 2014)

Printed in Canada